MARKSMANSHIP SIMPLIFIED

AN OBJECTIVE-BASED APPROACH TO SUPERIOR SHOOTING

Copyright© 2023

All rights reserved. No part of this publication may be reproduced, stored in a retrieval system or transmitted by any means — electronic, mechanical, photocopy, recording or otherwise — without first obtaining written permission from the author.

Printed in the United States.

ISBN 978-1-7341025-5-0

Marksmanship Simplified

First Printing, 2023.

Written by George Harris.

Edited by Carla Dickmann and Frank Jastrzembski.

Designed by Kelly Welke.

Illustrations by Jason Braun.

Photography by Ken Wangler, Kurt Adams, Daniel Acker and Keith Kamikawa. Other photos licensed for use.

SAFETY NOTE: While conducting live-fire, a shooter should wear proper safety equipment at all times. Any images in this book that show a shooter handling or otherwise using a firearm without the proper personal protection equipment were taken with firearms that had been cleared and used for dry-fire purposes only.

FOREWORD

George Harris wants everyone to be a better shooter. Period. Full stop.

In truth, I could stop writing this foreword with that line and it would be complete. It would also embrace a concept George has stressed over the years: Simple is good.

That simple idea was one of the driving principles behind his work at the SIG Sauer Academy, where he was instrumental in creating the first curriculum and infusing the Academy with the values that have made it one of the finest firearms training centers in the world. While he has moved on from SIG and the Academy, he has not stopped training shooters.

George has told me repeatedly over the years, "If the muzzle is pointed at the target when the shot is fired, the bullet will hit the target. It's just that simple."

He would then go on to explain that one needs sights to accurately orient the muzzle to the target. He would remember to add, "You must then operate the trigger without adding any additional movement to the muzzle." Then he would describe and demonstrate the "Wall Drill," which is designed to bring your focus to the front sight while you operate the trigger smoothly.

Before long, we would be involved in a 20-minute conversation touching on everything from grip to head position to sight picture to the importance of trigger operation. George would break down each element to its simplest parts, then combine them to show how they all worked together to improve accuracy. Every time he and I speak or correspond, I learn something new.

And it has been that way for something close to 15 years now.

For whatever reason, when I first met George, he decided I had something to offer the firearms community and began making time for me when I had questions. I had lots of questions. Before too long, we weren't just acquaintances meeting once a year at SHOT Show; we'd become good friends, and I'm the better man for it.

To say that George Harris has had an impact on the shooting public would be a gross understatement. But to talk, in his presence, about the impact he has had would most certainly make him uncomfortable. He is humble and talks without pretense on myriad topics.

The coolest thing about being a magazine editor and knowing George is that when I don't know where to turn for a bit of information or piece of institutional knowledge, he can immediately point me in the right direction. He knows everyone. He also knows about everything from historical firearms design to modern manufacturing techniques and continues to advise some of the biggest names in the industry, humbly adding a phrase like, "I am just the conduit."

But this is a book about pistol shooting. Specifically, it is about how to improve your pistol marksmanship skills. As George is so fond of saying, "The purpose of shooting is hitting."

It's just that simple: If you are going to fire a gun, the goal should be that you hit your target consistently. Period. Full stop.

George Harris has made a career helping people do just that, and I am proud to say that he has helped me improve every aspect of my life in the shooting sports. This book is a must-read for anyone who wants to shoot better. I am so happy to help my friend get his ideas on paper.

All you need to do now is read this book, orient the muzzle to the target and operate the trigger without adding any additional movement to the muzzle. It's just that simple, and simple is good.

— Kevin Michalowski, Executive Editor, *Concealed Carry Magazine*

CONTENTS

INTRODUCTION — 1

CHAPTER 1
SAFETY AND SUCCESS — 4
- Muzzle-Target Relationship — 6
- Off and On Target — 6

CHAPTER 2
THE ESSENTIALS — 8
- Muzzle Management — 10
- Trigger-Finger Discipline — 12
- Sight Alignment and Sight Picture — 13

CHAPTER 3
OBJECTIVE-BASED TRAINING — 16
- What's the Difference? — 19
- Stance: Doctrine-Based — 20
- Stance: Objective-Based — 22
- Integrating the Brain and Eyes — 23
- Mental-Visual Focus — 24
- Dry-Firing — 25

CHAPTER 4
COMMUNICATION — 28
- What, How, Why — 30
- Analogical Teaching — 31
- Objectives Versus Steps — 33
- Point, Pull, Hit — 34

CHAPTER 5
MENTAL FACTORS — 36
- Self-Preservation Response — 38
- Conscious Mind — 43
- Subconscious Mind — 44
- OODA Loop — 48

CHAPTER 6
VISUAL FACTORS — 50
- Iron Sights — 52
- Mini Red-Dot Sights — 55
- Eye Dominance — 57
- Central Vision — 60
- Peripheral Vision — 61

CHAPTER 7
BIOMECHANICAL FACTORS — 64
- Different Shapes and Sizes — 66
- Employing Natural Attributes — 66
- Building Fundamentals — 67

CHAPTER 8
DELIVERING A GOOD SHOT — 84
- See — 86
- Feel — 89
- Think — 94

CHAPTER 9
THE DIFFERENT DISCIPLINES 96
- Precision Marksmanship 98
- Combat and Defensive Marksmanship 100
- Recreational Marksmanship 104

CHAPTER 10
THE IMPORTANCE OF GOOD EQUIPMENT 106
- Safety Gear 108
- Guns and Ammo 111
- Sights 114
- Trigger 114
- Operational Verification 115
- Additional Accessories 117

CHAPTER 11
DIAGNOSTICS AND TROUBLESHOOTING 118
- Involuntary Movement 120
- Listening to and Feeling the Gun 123
- Trigger Jerk 125
- Wall Drill 128
- 3N1 Drill 129
- Ball and Dummy Drill 130
- Five-and-Five Drill 131
- Double-Action to Single-Action Transition Drill 131
- Validating Front-Sight Focus 132
- Shoot the Shape Drill 134
- Simplified Sight Picture 134
- Correcting Grip Deficiencies 135
- Three-Hand Drill 137
- Limp Wristing 138
- Stablizing the Muzzle 139
- Vision Anomalies 141
- Lack of Visual Clarity 143
- Mini Red-Dot Sights 144
- Physiological and Psychological Considerations 146

CHAPTER 12
DRILLS TO ATTAIN & RETAIN PROFICIENCY 152
- Wall Drill 155
- Bullet Hole Drill 157
- Shoot the Shape Drill 158
- Walk Back Drill 158
- Reset Drill 159
- Now Drill 160
- Precision to Point Transition Drill 161
- One-Handed Shooting Drills 163
- Support-Hand-Only Drills 164

CHAPTER 13
PATHS TO IMPROVEMENT 166
- Training Approach 168
- Brain, Vision and Body 169
- Diversification 170
- Detecting Deficiencies 172
- Pay It Forward 173

INTRODUCTION

Marksmanship Simplified is a holistic approach to accurate shooting that applies the essentials necessary for individual success in shooting a handgun. These essentials are derived from combining visual, mental and biomechanical factors to maximize a shooter's performance. These concepts of adult learning are objective-based as opposed to doctrine-based, which permits a shooter to learn and retain the subject matter with minimal time and effort. Since each thought and action is simple, easy to understand and relatively easy to reproduce, this approach to shooter development and improvement is incredibly successful.

Beginning with the foundational principles of safety and success, accomplished by the two simple procedures of muzzle management and trigger-finger discipline, a reader will recognize the simplicity and application of the guidelines presented throughout the book.

Comparisons interspersed between conventional training methodologies and the alternatives presented in the text answer what might serve the reader best and why. Realizing that individuals learn in many different ways, multiple methods are offered to streamline the process of adding new knowledge and techniques to a shooter's abilities.

The concepts of objective-based training and analogous training are introduced as alternative methods of streamlining student understanding through simple, understandable communication and direction techniques.

By merging a comprehensive and in-depth study of human vision and biomechanical factors with the mental aspects of shooting, an individual can develop a performance plan specific to his or her needs. By learning what is required in order to make a good shot — what a shooter needs to see, feel and think — the individual can identify and cultivate a plan that leads to the desired performance.

Marksmanship — the ability to achieve shot placement in the desired location on a target and within the constraints of time — often varies with the requirements of a shooter's discipline. The study of precision marksmanship, combat marksmanship, competitive shooting, hunting and recreational shooting shows that each has specific and unique requirements. Once familiar with these requirements, a shooter will be able to implement the best actions and techniques for the challenges that arise in any of the disciplines.

An important and valuable part of this comprehensive compilation of information is diagnosing and troubleshooting deficiencies. These drills and analyses enable a shooter or an instructor to identify and permanently correct bad habits and practices interfering with an individual's shooting process.

Included are paths to improvement, which pave the way for enhanced shooter performance. Perhaps as important, sharing knowledge and experiences with other shooters — including prospective ones — helps to increase the overall number of safe and successful shooters.

Simple but necessary sustainment exercises are included to provide the practitioner with an easy plan of action when at the range. This is opposed to a shooter going to the range and shooting at targets with no specific purpose or objective.

A treatise on marksmanship would not be complete without mentioning the value of having the right type of quality equipment to support a shooter's efforts in both safety and success. In keeping with the original concept of the book, simplicity of equipment and accessories serves the shooter best in accomplishing a specific objective.

A reader should feel encouraged to highlight and reread portions of the material as the concept of safety with success takes shape and becomes easy to implement. The phrase "everything you need, nothing you don't" is applicable here.

Marksmanship Simplified will be the first point of reference when a question regarding shooting a handgun arises.

CHAPTER 1
SAFETY AND SUCCESS

Whenever a firearm is present, especially if someone is handling it, safety should be the No. 1 priority. A constant awareness of where the muzzle of the gun is pointed and the relationship of the trigger finger to the trigger will provide rudimentary safety in almost any situation.

While there are many facets of firearms-handling etiquette — enough to fill a book — muzzle management and trigger-finger discipline will ensure that no personal injury or property damage occurs while someone is handling a firearm. The simplicity of learning and practicing those two things takes the mystery out of handling and shooting a gun — especially for someone who is new to firearms.

All other aspects of firearms safety, such as storage, maintenance, handling, transporting, carrying, shooting and any other activity, can be traced back to muzzle management and trigger-finger discipline.

MUZZLE-TARGET RELATIONSHIP

Success, when related to shooting a firearm, can be simply described as hitting the target where and when the shooter desires.

Using a bit of logic and reason, it's not hard to understand that the position of the firearm's muzzle in relation to the target determines where the bullet will end up. If the gun is pointed at the target when it is fired, it is likely that the bullet will hit the target. If the gun is pointed somewhere other than the target when discharge occurs, success in hitting the target is unlikely.

To complete the act of hitting the target, the muzzle must be in the correct proximity to the target and the shot has to be released without affecting the muzzle's relationship to the target. This is done by moving the trigger to fire the gun without moving the muzzle's position as it relates to the target.

With all things considered, if the gun's muzzle is pointed at the target when the trigger is pulled, it will likely result in a hit.

OFF AND ON TARGET

Muzzle management and trigger-finger discipline, when a shooter practices them as described, will yield both safety and success when that individual is handling or using a firearm.

Keep in mind that no firearm in good working order will arbitrarily fire by itself. A shooter should keep the trigger finger away from the trigger until he or she has pointed the muzzle of the gun at the target and has made the decision to shoot. Then and only then should the shooter pull the trigger to fire the gun without moving the muzzle off the target.

A simple way to develop a safe shooting habit is for the shooter to remember: "On target, on trigger. Off target, off trigger."

This means that if the shooter has the sights, and therefore the muzzle, pointed at the target and has made the decision to shoot that target, it is then appropriate to touch and smoothly pull the trigger with

the trigger finger to release the shot. At any other time, when the muzzle is not pointed at a target and there is no intention to fire the gun, the shooter's trigger finger must not be in contact with the trigger and should instead be extended straight forward, resting against the side of the gun.

The two most important things a new shooter (and even an experienced shooter) must remember is that muzzle management and trigger-finger discipline are the key principles of safe and successful shooting.

CHAPTER 2
THE ESSENTIALS

Marksmanship is defined as skill in shooting. The objective of shooting is placing a shot on an intended target.

There are two actions that must happen for a shooter to meet that objective. The first is to stabilize the muzzle in the proper proximity to the target so that the shot and the intended hit location will coincide at impact of the shot. The second is to pull the trigger, firing the shot, without altering or affecting the muzzle's relationship to the target.

These two factors are indisputable.

If one (or both) of these factors is absent, the shooter will not achieve the objective. It's as simple as that.

A shooter — new or experienced — must understand and apply a few foundational principles in order to meet the goal of hitting the intended target. These are simple procedures that form a solid foundation on which a shooter can build and to which a shooter can add as his or her goals expand to more specific directions.

MUZZLE MANAGEMENT

Starting with the basic shooting platform, typically referred to as "stance," the overall objective is to be balanced, which allows mobility and facilitates muzzle stability on the target. Since humans come in all shapes and sizes, there is no one-size-fits-all position that meets this objective. If a shooter can stand vertically — holding the gun with arms extended toward the target — and maintain balance and the ability to move forward, backward and to either side, his or her center of gravity will automatically accommodate this position. Then, with progress, the shooter can make minor adjustments to the overall platform to help further maintain muzzle stability on the target.

Holding the gun, most often referred to as "grip," should be natural and simple. The objective is for the shooter to position the gun in the web of the dominant hand so that the barrel points toward the target (as if the index finger were "pointing" at the target). This utilizes the shooter's natural attribute of eye-hand coordination — the ability to point the finger at anything to which the eye is attracted — to orient the muzzle's position on or close to the target.

The caveat here is whether the shooter can reach the trigger with the gun positioned in this manner. Fitting the gun to the shooter's hand is important and will be covered in greater detail later. Ideally, if the index finger can establish full contact across the face of the trigger, the shooter will achieve proper trigger manipulation.

It is important that the gun sit low and tight against the web of the shooter's hand so that he or she can control the pushback, or recoil, while firing.

The thumb of the dominant hand should rest on the opposite side of the gun from the trigger finger, forming a pocket in which the gun can rest.

The middle, ring and pinkie fingers should wrap naturally around the grip of the gun, with the middle finger in close contact with the trigger guard portion of the frame. Grip pressure is somewhat subjective but should be firm and sustainable while a shooter expends all of the rounds in the pistol's magazine. The objective is to exert enough pressure on the gun to prevent slippage or movement of the gun in the hand through the complete cycle of firing, but not so much as to restrict the movement of the trigger finger.

It is recommended that the shooter use both hands to grip the gun whenever possible.

If the shooter uses the non-dominant (support) hand, it should be positioned to provide maximum contact and support on the grip and frame. The heels of the hands should be positioned tightly together, with the support-side thumb parallel to and touching the bottom of the dominant-side thumb. Both thumbs should be pointing forward, parallel to the barrel, if possible. The fingers of the support hand will overlap the fingers of the dominant hand, with the index finger tight under the trigger guard to provide vertical support. Grip pressure from the support hand should be slightly greater than the pressure from the dominant hand, ensuring that sufficient friction between the grip of the gun and the hands is maintained to guarantee total control of the gun up to and through firing a complete complement of ammunition as required for the shooting exercise.

The objective of gripping the gun is that the muzzle rise vertically and settle back to the same location on the target each time a shooter fires it. Minor adjustments of grip pressure and the placement of the gun in the hands will accomplish this objective.

 PREFERABLE
 ACCEPTABLE
 ACCEPTABLE

TRIGGER-FINGER DISCIPLINE

Trigger manipulation is the most important aspect of firing any gun. Improper trigger manipulation can spoil an otherwise perfectly developed shot at the final instant before the bullet exits the muzzle.

Once the shooter has made the decision to shoot and has the gun pointed at and stabilized on the target, pulling the trigger is the last essential act to achieve a successful hit.

The trigger must be moved through its full range of motion to release the shot toward the target.

To do this, pressure from the index finger must be applied on the trigger, parallel to the frame, with no other influence or pressure from the hands or movement from any other part of the body.

This action may be performed fast or slow — as long as there is minimal to no effect on the relationship of the muzzle of the gun to the target.

Trigger reset is a secondary consideration to trigger manipulation. Trigger reset is the control of the trigger forward after a shot has been fired. It reconnects the

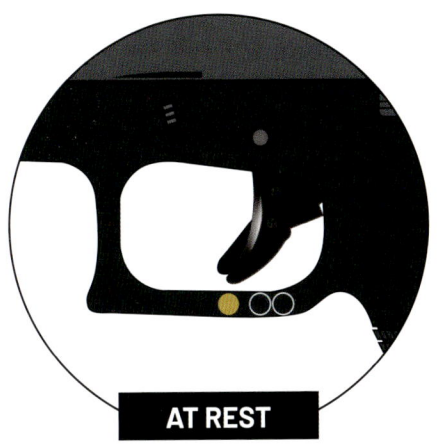

AT REST
The trigger is fully forward.

BREAK POINT
This is the point at which the striker is released and the gun fires.

RESET POINT
The trigger resets at this point and can be pulled again (without letting the trigger travel all the way forward to the rest position). Note the minimal difference between the reset and break points.

internal firing mechanism, enabling the next shot to be fired. Ideally, the trigger finger should maintain contact with and control the movement of the trigger forward to reset as the muzzle rises off the target in recoil. Once reset is achieved, and as the muzzle is settling back to the desired location on the target, the shooter should reapply trigger pressure to fire another shot. The shooter should perform multiple shots as a smooth, fluid sequence of events. Once firing is complete, the shooter should remove the trigger finger from the trigger and extend it along the frame, above the trigger, until firing resumes.

To promote a more complete understanding of trigger manipulation, an analogy could be drawn to the operation of an accelerator or brake pedal on a motor vehicle. The key to well-controlled acceleration or deceleration of a motor vehicle is smooth, fluid pressure on the pedal as opposed to erratic, convulsive movement.

SIGHT ALIGNMENT AND SIGHT PICTURE

Close in importance to trigger control is how to use the sights in the best possible manner to hit the target.

Sights are easy to integrate into the shooting process, provided a shooter understands why they are on the gun in the first place and how the eyes work naturally to best use those sights to achieve a goal.

The shooter must take advantage of the natural ability of eye-hand coordination to get the muzzle of the gun in the direction of the target. The sights are used to fine-tune or more precisely place the position of the muzzle to a specific location on the target. The more precisely the sights are aligned, the tighter and more consistent the hits are on the target. That's why it's so important for the shooter's eyes to be focused on the sights the second the bullet leaves the muzzle and heads toward the target.

A shooter can easily confirm whether his or her eyes are open and focused on the sights at the moment of discharge. If so, the shooter will notice the muzzle flash and blast around the front sight. The movement of the ejected brass between the front and rear sights will also be visually apparent.

Sight alignment can be made simple by understanding that the human eye naturally centers objects when they're viewed through an opening. Most handguns have a round night sight, painted dot or colored fiber optic in the front sight to draw the eye's attention, so it's easy for the eye to center the attractive dot in the rear-sight notch when the shooter views the dot through the notch. All the shooter needs to do is be aware that the front sight is being viewed through the window of the rear-sight notch to achieve the necessary alignment.

Sight picture is different from sight alignment in that it adds a target to the equation.

Again, using the eye's natural ability to center objects with amazing precision, sight picture can be simplified by superimposing the dot in the front sight, as viewed through the rear-sight notch, on the center of the target for a successful hit.

The shooter must execute both sight alignment and sight picture consistently to achieve acceptable accuracy. The goal is to obtain shot groups that tend to be round and decrease in size as proficiency is gained. A shooter can adjust the group placement on the target, as desired, by adjusting the sights. However, it is pointless to adjust the sights prior to being able to shoot acceptable groups.

CRUCIAL TO SUCCESS

These essential elements of marksmanship will allow a shooter to attain remarkable skills in hitting a target. These skills can then be perfected and improved as the shooter's goals become more focused. Competitive shooting, defensive shooting, hunting and just plinking for recreation each has unique requirements that may require specialized training and practice to maximize a shooter's performance.

CHAPTER 3
OBJECTIVE-BASED TRAINING

Traditional marksmanship training is typically taught as a series of specific topics using a "building block" or "one-size-fits-all" approach that leaves little room for flexibility. The instructor usually delivers the information to students with the expectation that they will be able to understand, retain and perform each point with some degree of proficiency. Rarely is there an effort to incorporate relatable, previously learned skills that could be beneficial to each student's understanding of the material. This methodology, sometimes referred to as "doctrine-based training," has been used for many years in the firearms community with enough success to be accepted as a standard means for teaching shooting.

However, some students find this methodology of being inundated with information overwhelming, and they fail to grasp the concepts as a result. Others find it overly complicated for long-term retention and quickly lose interest. Those who are genuinely interested in the subject struggle with this type of training and may need to receive the information in a different way. An instructor should be able to explain why the training is relevant to each student's individual interests and how it might be adjusted to better meet that individual's particular needs. The instructor should consider employing alternate methods of getting the message across or risks sending students away without learning or retaining much of what they heard.

Alternative methods of communicating the necessary information and techniques exist in multiple forms. The primary criterion is that they are simple, make sense and are relatively easy for students to reproduce. They should be equally as effective as — if not superior to

— the use of conventional training methods in educating and training shooters to excel in their chosen disciplines.

An alternative to doctrine-based training that could be used as a replacement methodology or in a complementary role is objective-based training.

WHAT'S THE DIFFERENCE?

What differentiates doctrine-based training from objective-based training is that the former involves a strict, detail-oriented, step-by-step method of achieving an outcome, while the latter presents the desired outcome in the beginning and offers students a degree of flexibility in how they accomplish a given task. Rather than being told what to do in great detail with the expectation of mirror-like duplication, students are told what they need to do with just enough detail necessary to perform the task in an acceptable manner. The use of previously learned skills and natural ability as it applies to the objective is suggested and encouraged. The techniques used in objective-based training streamline the learning process for students, leaving more time for an instructor to share additional information or for students to practice the material they've learned.

Some examples of conventional doctrine-based training methods typically used in teaching shooting skills are listed in this chapter. They will be followed by suggested alternative methods that require less time and effort on each student's part to meet a desired result. Once a student's foundational skill is firmly in place, he or she can easily add additional methods as applicable to the specific discipline at hand.

The idea is to get a baseline established by maximizing the use of a student's natural attributes and previously acquired skills and then refine those qualities as necessary to meet the desired goals.

STANCE: DOCTRINE-BASED

An instructor usually spends a significant amount of time on stance since it is regarded as the foundation of a student's evolution to successful shooting. The message delivered is that the shooter's feet should be slightly more than shoulder-width apart, with the dominant-side foot slightly offset to the rear — similar to a boxer's stance. An alternative would be to have the shoot-

DOCTRINE-BASED

[*dok-trin-beyst*]

A strict, detail-oriented, step-by-step method of achieving an outcome. Students are told what to do in great detail with the expectation of mirror-like duplication.

OBJECTIVE-BASED

[*uhb-jek-tiv-beyst*]

A training method where the desired outcome is presented in the beginning and offers students a degree of flexibility in how they accomplish a given task. Students are told what they need to do with just enough detail necessary to perform the task in an acceptable manner.

er's feet slightly more than shoulder-width apart, side by side, in line, and perpendicular to the target.

Balance for either stance is described as distributing approximately 70 percent of the body weight over the balls of the feet, with the remaining weight supported by the heels. Moving upward, the knees should be slightly bent, allowing the hips to be positioned forward over the balls of the feet for proper weight distribution. Continuing further up the body, the upper torso and shoulders should angle forward of the hips to resist the recoil produced by the gun. The arms are typically extended, parallel to the ground, with the elbows and wrists locked to resist the gun's recoil. This arm position is usually commensurate with the side-by-side foot position. An alternative arm position could be extending and locking the dominant arm, with the support arm flexed slightly at the elbow, exerting a push-pull pressure on the grip of the gun. This arm position is most often recommended when a shooter uses the offset boxer's stance foot position. The head is positioned so that the sights of the gun can be aligned and positioned relative to the target when the arms and hands are extended toward the target.

STANCE: OBJECTIVE-BASED

The alternative or objective description of stance can be described in two words: "balance" and "mobility." If a shooter is balanced and is mobile in any of the 360 degrees available, he or she can meet the objective of stabilizing the muzzle of the gun on the target, which is a key component of hitting the target.

Keep in mind that every shooter is not created physically equal. There are differences in size, weight and shape that cause variances in flexibility, range of movement and center of gravity. Using specific terms of foot position and body posture to direct a group of students of all shapes and sizes into a typical standing shooting position while holding a gun on a target is likely not going to be as effective for some as it is for others.

On the other hand, having each student stand naturally, point the gun at the target and then take a few steps left, right, forward and backward will allow the student to determine a balanced shooting position that will allow the muzzle of the firearm to be stabilized on the target to the maximum of his or her ability, which is the objective of a shooting stance.

Practicing balance and mobility as previously described gives each shooter a good foundation from which to begin. In some cases, this is all a student will need to meet success. As the student gravitates to a more specific discipline that may require more detailed attention, he or she can make refinements to better meet the overall objective. Regardless of the path the student travels, the objective should still be the same: muzzle stability on the target at the moment the shot is released.

INTEGRATING THE BRAIN AND EYES

Aside from the mechanics of shooting — upon which most traditional methods of firearms training are based — objective-based training holistically integrates the brain and the eyes along with the biomechanical aspects of shooting.

A primary differentiator between traditional training and objective-based training is eliminating detrimental habits and actions before they ever get started. Chapters 5 and 11 will discuss — in depth — how a shooter can overcome the self-preservation response, which plays an important role in curbing bad habits. The self-preservation response is an innate reaction to danger, loud noises and the perception of possible physical damage to the body — particularly the eyes. Each time a gun fires, it makes a loud noise, and the recoil moves the pistol toward the eyes. Unless the noise and recoil are dealt with in the very early stages of firearms usage, the brain takes measures to protect the body from them, resulting in preempting both when the trigger is pulled, which moves the muzzle off the target prior to the bullet's exit, usually resulting in a miss. This phenomenon is referred to as a "flinch" or "trigger jerk," among other names. If left unchecked, it will become a lifelong challenge for a shooter.

Conventional trainers suggest that by shooting thousands of rounds, a shooter can overcome the involuntary movements of flinching, jerking and blinking.

An objective-based trainer can eliminate these problems — before they even start — in about 30 minutes.

Traditional firearms training teaches the hard-and-fast rule that the gun's front sight must be the point of focus for accurate shooting. But this is only part of the equation. In many cases, a shooter, regardless of skill level, cannot consistently describe the sight picture and the visual perception of what takes place each time the gun fires. Often, a shooter who has been trained in the traditional manner will close his or her eyes while delivering the shot and not even know it.

That same individual, when trained using an objective-based methodology, learns to self-diagnose the visual experience each time the gun fires. This makes it easy to detect and correct deficiencies as well as validate shot placement on the target without viewing the target. By answering a few simple questions, the shooter can self-correct on the go.

The matter of whether a shooter's eyes are open at the moment of discharge can be addressed by answering the following: Does the shooter observe brass leaving the ejection port or, in the case of a revolver, the flash at the barrel-cylinder gap when the gun fires? It is undeniable that one of these things happens every time the shooter fires the gun — and it happens between the front sight and rear sight, which must be in visual alignment for an accurate shot. If the shooter's eyes are open and focused on the sights of the gun, wouldn't it be reasonable to recognize the movement of the ejected brass or the flash at the barrel-cylinder gap in his or her peripheral vision each time the gun fires?

Understanding human eyes and vision can be tremendously beneficial to both the instructor and the student.

MENTAL-VISUAL FOCUS

Another difference between traditional and objective-based training techniques is that the latter utilizes visual input to make decisions in milliseconds by providing input to the brain, which in turn controls the actions of the body to perform at the levels necessary to achieve the desired results.

Mental and visual focus are typically treated separately in doctrine-based training.

An example would be how the trigger is operated to fire the gun. It is often described as "squeezing" the trigger to the rear with slow and steady pressure until a surprise break takes place. It takes a lot of mental fortitude to accomplish this even once — much less multiple times — without affecting the relationship of the muzzle to the target.

Equally as important as trigger control is how the sights are addressed in relation to the target. Sight alignment and sight picture have to be repeatable and consistent in order to achieve the expected impacts on the target. A shooter achieves optimal performance by focusing on the front sight, maintaining the correct sight picture until the gun fires and then starting all over again as quickly as possible if multiple shots are necessary.

The conundrum is deciding the most important aspect to which the shooter should devote the most focus, assuming that total focus is a singular action for a human to practice at any given time.

Objective-based training offers a holistic solution by combining visual input with biomechanical action, coordinated by the brain, to fire each shot consistently and within the capability of the shooter and the equipment used.

It's a very simple process: The sight picture incorporates the center of the shape of the target the individual is shooting, utilizing the natural ability to find the center of any object with either central or peripheral vision. The eye should be focused, hard, on the front sight, and the trigger finger should be in firm contact with the trigger. The student must mentally focus on pulling the front sight — conceptually as if it were on a rail — through the rear-sight notch in perfect alignment with the movement of the trigger (as though the two were connected).

This combines the two essential components of precision shot delivery into one simple process that is easily attainable. The shooter ends up giving the same amount of effort to sight alignment and trigger control individually and collectively by using this technique. An additional byproduct is that this technique occupies the efforts of the brain, eyes and hands and, as a result, there is little room for distraction to interfere with the shot-delivery process.

DRY-FIRING

Perhaps one difference of the highest magnitude between traditional and objective-based training methods is the practice of dry-firing. Dry-firing is designed to replicate the act of live-firing but without the noise and recoil. Traditional dry-fire techniques usually concentrate on single areas of shot delivery, such as trigger control, sight alignment and how to hold the gun for minimal movement and maximum stability. Occasionally, dry-fire is combined with a live-fire exercise, such as the "Ball and Dummy Drill," to help with deficiencies in controlling the trigger.

Using the concepts of objective-based training, the "Wall Drill" employs every asset necessary to deliver what the shooter needs to see, feel and think in delivering a good shot. Going back to the premise that the objective of shooting is to hit a target and that the way to do that is to stabilize the muzzle on the target and pull the trigger without affecting the muzzle's stability, the "Wall Drill" is an excellent conditioning tool for an individual to practice in order to improve and perfect shooting performance.

With the muzzle at the wall, the eye is forced to stay on the sights through the fall of the hammer or release of the striker. Any deviation in the sight alignment through the full pull of the trigger indicates that the operation of the trigger is not as smooth as it could be. It could also mean that grip pressure from one or both hands is inconsistent from shot to shot. In either case, both should be considered when the sights move during a dry-fire shot. The mental game of shooting can be improved by conditioning the brain to signal the finger to pull the trigger without conscious thought when the sight picture is at its best. This is the purest form of shot delivery and is rarely, if ever, seen in traditional training.

The "Wall Drill" is a foundational staple of developing good shooting habits as well as an excellent diagnostic tool that uses the three essentials of biomechanics, vision and mental processing to guide a shooter's evolution to continued improvement.

OBJECTIVE-BASED TRAINING BENEFITS

These are but a few of the many differences between traditional methods of firearms instruction and objective-based training methods. The subsequent chapters go into depth and detail in explaining the benefits of objective-based training, how it works alone or in conjunction with other training methodologies, and why it is important to the advancement of all shooters — regardless of their disciplines or reasons for shooting.

CHAPTER 4
COMMUNICATION

The way knowledge and skill are transferred to others starts with communicating a concept or idea. The manner in which that concept or idea is communicated determines the effectiveness and permanence of the information transfer.

In teaching and learning marksmanship skills, particularly using conventional training methods, often too much information is delivered at once for most people to assimilate.

Consider that the average human can cognitively process five to seven bits of information simultaneously under normal circumstances. When time constraints or elements of urgency are introduced, the amount of information that can be cognitively processed diminishes. For this reason, the learning process must be kept simple and succinct.

Marksmanship, like any other eye-hand coordinated task, requires contributions from the senses of sight, touch and sound, coordinated by the brain, where they combine to achieve the desired outcome. The means by which the information is communicated determines the immediate and long-term performance level of an individual learning a new skill.

The very best teachers convey a message not only in a way in which their students will understand the information or task but also so that it won't be misunderstood. It leaves no doubt as to the application and use of the message, leaving little room for further discussion.

The questions of what, how and why as related to the subject matter must be clear, concise and indisputable to be successful.

WHAT, HOW, WHY

Related to marksmanship, regardless of whether it is defensive, competitive or casual, the "what" is how a shooter defines success. Success in marksmanship is striking the target where and when the shooter intends to hit it.

The "how" can be distilled down to stabilizing the muzzle on the target while pulling the trigger to cause discharge without affecting the muzzle's relationship to the target. It should be noted that "stabilize" is defined as controlling the muzzle's movement so there is the least amount of motion possible. (It won't ever be motionless without some kind of mechanical support.)

The "why" is simply how the shooter benefits from the action. It is to successfully achieve the "what" in the triad of what, how and why. If the objective of marksmanship is hitting the target when and where the shooter intends, and if successful hits are made within those parameters, the shooter accomplished the learning component and practical performance.

Presenting the what, how and why of marksmanship without acronyms or abbreviations makes it clear to anyone who has a basic awareness of gun nomenclature that the primary concerns for safety — muzzle management and trigger-finger discipline — are the same actions required for success. A shooter can achieve both safety and success with any firearm by practicing awareness of where the muzzle is pointed at all times and of the relationship of the index finger to the trigger.

Communicating objectives and expectations in concise and simple terms is especially important. This is because many of us are conditioned early in life to take in bits of information, such as "A, B and C" or "1, 2 and 3." Once the foundation is solid, more can be added; however, too much information at once tends to dilute or even eliminate the essentials necessary for successfully accomplishing the task.

When a statement or action cannot be questioned, it is indisputable. It is easily accepted as fact with no discussion necessary. Information that isn't completely clear or that can be questioned is distracting when it comes to learning and performing a marksmanship skill. Unclear communication interferes with a shooter's acceptance and retention of information.

In the example mentioned earlier, it would be difficult to argue against the probability of hitting a target if the muzzle is pointed at it when the bullet leaves the barrel.

An individual easily retains information if the message is presented in a concise and simple way, is indisputable, and is easy to replicate with a minimum of repetitions in a practical exercise. Marksmanship is made easy when it's presented this way.

ANALOGICAL TEACHING

An exceptionally useful technique of communicating information that streamlines the learning process is called "analogical teaching." This technique uses an analogy to connect shooting to a commonly known and practiced skill with which a student may already be familiar.

Assuming that most of the people being taught marksmanship can drive a motor vehicle, it is easy to make an analogy between driving a car and shooting a gun.

Perhaps the most prevalent and valuable analogy between the two is comparing the movement of the gun's trigger to the accelerator movement of a motor vehicle. Both require smooth, fluid movement as well as control in both directions by way of constant contact to drive or shoot in the most efficient and consistent manner. A person doesn't typically drive a motor vehicle by abruptly smashing the accelerator to the floor to move from a stationary position, quickly removing the foot from the accelerator as soon as the vehicle starts moving and then proceeding to do it over again until he or she finally reaches a stopping point. Suggesting that manipulating the trigger of a gun is similar to operating the accelerator on a motor vehicle will likely smooth out a shooter's trigger jerk and other issues associated with trigger movement that are not conducive to good marksmanship.

Communicating using analogical teaching methods and techniques is significantly enhanced when instructors get to know the individuals being taught the concepts of marksmanship prior to class. It sometimes helps to know what some of their past experiences have been, enabling them to learn through a comparison to information with which they're already familiar. Often these experiences have similarities to shooting and marksmanship that can be used to increase the understanding of the shooting technique.

Another example is the eye focus of a golfer who is making a long drive down the fairway. For a golfer to make a successful drive, his or her eyes must be intently focused on the back of the golf ball until the club contacts the ball and the ball leaves the tee. The same thing applies to the front sight of a pistol, where hard focus is necessary until the bullet exits the muzzle. In either case, both the visual input of eye focus and the mental aspect of follow-through are emphasized, which are essential to repeatable success (in shot delivery or driving the ball down the fairway).

It is important to have an analogy when communicating any of the basic skills required for marksmanship development.

How a shooter should hold or grip a handgun, for example, can be directly correlated to driving a nail with a hammer. If an individual grips the hammer too tightly, the accuracy in hitting the nail without bending it significantly diminishes. Conversely, holding the hammer too loosely will result in losing control of the hammer. Like the hammer, the handgun has a "sweet spot," or range of grip pressure, that will yield the best results of muzzle control and recoil recovery.

Analogies help with the understanding of what an individual needs to see and feel to be able to deliver an acceptable shot to the target. Once this understanding is in place and accepted, the point is embedded in the individual's memory for retrieval when the application requires it.

Analogical teaching requires an instructor to have experience in a variety of fields in order to effectively compare shooting to an entirely different skill. This helps the instructor communicate the simplicity of shooting to a greater number of people by practicing methods of performance already familiar to them. Effective communication is essential in introducing developmental skills and elevating each student's performance by refining the technique of delivering an accurate shot.

OBJECTIVES VERSUS STEPS

Teaching marksmanship by using objectives instead of a series of steps leading to a specific goal is not new. However, it is not often used in elevating the proficiency of students receiving firearms training. This is largely because only a few trainers who taught marksmanship in the past were bold enough to break with common practices and try something different.

For many years, conventional firearms training was doctrine-based, regardless of whether an individual was learning to shoot for competition, personal defense, hunting or plinking in the backyard. Entry-level, intermediate and advanced training usually involved showering students with such a large variety of techniques and absolutes that they were overloaded with information, which inhibited retention and performance. The conventional concept was that no matter how much information to which a student was exposed, that student would retain at least some of it. Theoretically, with enough repetition, a student would improve over time, even if it took hundreds or thousands of rounds.

Invariably, some students eventually improved, while others gave up in frustration because they weren't fortunate enough to pick up the essential ideas and techniques necessary for success.

Fortunately, there were a few forward-thinking individuals in the firearms training world who stepped outside of the realm of conventional training. These trainers knew there must be more-effective ways of coaxing performance out of their students in a shorter period of time than by using the conventional "I talk, you listen" and "Do this, don't do that" methods of teaching shooting skills.

Studying how humans learn, retain information and perform revealed that flooding students with massive amounts of information in the hope that something will stick doesn't work all that well. In fact, comprehensive academic studies about adult learning suggest that under ideal conditions, five to seven bits of information is the limit of cognitive processing for the average human. These studies also found that this number diminished when factors of stress were introduced.

For instance, when a student is learning the basics of marksmanship — foot position, arm position, head position and angle of the torso (with an emphasis on recoil resistance) — his or her cognitive-processing ability is essentially "used up" on stance alone. When sight alignment, sight picture, trigger control, left-handed grip, right-handed grip, breathing and coordinating all of them to fall into the right sequence come into play, the maximum cognitive capacity for the average human has been exceeded.

It should be noted that information or a skill intended to be committed to the subconscious level must first be cognitively processed before it transitions to the subconscious mind, where it is permanently stored for future use. Too much information requiring conscious or cognitive processing actually inhibits the learning process of permanency in the subconscious mind.

These facts necessitated rethinking the approach to making efficient and effective behavioral changes to help individuals become successful shooters — particularly in a specific discipline with a single type of firearm. This inspired some instructors to break down the methods of teaching to two or three bits of information, ensuring their students understood and could mimic what they demonstrated before building on the foundational skills further.

This led to identifying a specific learning objective a student should know and be able to do after the lesson, followed by what was necessary to accomplish that objective. Teaching in this objective-based manner simplifies and enhances learning as well as retention of the subject matter.

POINT, PULL, HIT

To start this process, the verbal explanation of the task needs to make sense to the student, be indisputable and be relatively easy to reproduce successfully within the time frame of the lesson (using a minimum number of steps).

A relevant example is how foundational levels of marksmanship can be taught using the method of objective-based training.

The objective of shooting, regardless of discipline or firearms type, is hitting the target. This is indisputable.

When it comes to a handgun and a single stationary target on a recreational range, the two things that are absolutely necessary to hit the target are to stabilize the muzzle on the target and to pull the trigger to fire the shot without negatively influencing the stability of the muzzle. Remember, "stabilize" means to hold the gun as still as possible for the time it takes to pull the trigger and fire the shot. An explanation that the gun won't be motionless is helpful since it is virtually impossible to keep most firearms perfectly still. It helps the shooter to execute a smooth trigger pull even though some movement may be evident.

It's literally point gun, pull trigger and hit target. It's simple and it works.

From this point, there are usually two paths to follow. If the shooter isn't having much success, it's easy to diagnose what's standing in the way. It's either failing to stabilize the muzzle on the target until the bullet exits the gun or mismanipulating the trigger, causing the muzzle to veer off the target by adding unnecessary motion to the gun. It's not difficult for an instructor to uncover what the student is doing, determine why it's happening and formulate a plan on how to fix it.

The other path is to build on the student's success in hitting the target by fine-tuning and enhancing previously learned skills. This is where the extras and adjustments can be introduced into the process.

From an objective-based perspective, teaching stance for personal defense and some types of competitive shooting is simple, makes sense, is easy to reproduce and is indisputable. The three key words are "balance," "mobility" and "stability." One leads to the other in that a shooter needs to be balanced to be mobile. Being stationary in a gunfight or in a tactical course of fire is not advantageous. Having the ability to move in any of the 360 degrees on demand ensures mobility. The balance that allows the mobility also helps in stabilizing the muzzle on the target, which lends itself to the overall objective of hitting the target.

DRAWING A PARALLEL

Objective-based training is a simple, straightforward and effective way to educate and train students. It gives students what they need to be successful, eliminating the unnecessary details that clog their minds and are rarely useful. It also allows students to bring previously learned skills from other venues, such as golf and other sports or life experiences, and apply them to shooting so that they can be successful. Many students already have the skills to be successful marksmen once the parallels have been introduced.

As an instructor or a student, consider stepping out of the box, identifying the objective and finding the simplest and most effective way to accomplish the goal. Keep in mind what is vital to achieve success. The simpler the message, the better.

The essentials of marksmanship are built from the foundational skills of managing the muzzle and moving the trigger without affecting the muzzle's relationship to the target. Additions can be made to these essentials as desired, but the foundation remains.

Success is indisputable!

CHAPTER 5
MENTAL FACTORS

It's no secret that the objective of shooting is hitting the intended target. Technically speaking, only two things need to happen to achieve this objective. The first is to stabilize the muzzle of the firearm on the target area. Since the muzzle of the firearm is the only place projectiles leave the gun to engage the target, it stands to reason that this is an absolute. The second is to cause the firearm to discharge without interfering with the muzzle's stability on the target. Herein lies the challenge for most shooters.

There have been countless studies conducted and articles written on how to help skill-deficient shooters. They range from mechanical solutions to technical explanations of the integrated act of shot delivery. Occasionally, there are explorations into the areas of psychology, physiology and vision that pique the interest of shooters intent on improving their performance. But unless there is a working knowledge of these areas and how they apply to precision marksmanship, the information is not very useful.

Over the years, the more successful trainers have learned that simplified training methods are one of the most effective means of elevating student performance in the least amount of time. Key questions that are often left unanswered in the training process are how and why a specific learning principle works to produce positive results. If shooters understand the whys and hows of the subject being taught, they are much more likely to use the information to their benefit.

The following commentary is not a simple rehash and review of mental training and shooting psychology but rather a blend of more than four decades of marksmanship training experience and academic validation provided by certified professionals in a variety of related fields. The individuals who contributed to the formulation of this material include government employees, military personnel, law enforcement officers and civilians — domestic and foreign and nonspecific to gender, race, religion, political affiliation or physical ability. They also range from novice to international record holder. Even though the concepts, ideas and methods have been proven many times over, studying them makes marksmanship training and marksmanship itself simple and easy to understand and reproduce with minimal effort and maximum results.

SELF-PRESERVATION RESPONSE

The No. 1 cause for a shooter's lack of success in marksmanship and shooting in general is the "self-preservation response." It is a protective mechanism built into the brain that is triggered when a loud noise or threat surprises the individual or happens unexpectedly. It is similar, but not identical, to the fight-or-flight response generated when a person recognizes danger.

The self-preservation response is a predominately innate and therefore natural response to the discharge of a firearm. It causes errant movement to the muzzle of a firearm slightly before or during the discharge of the gun, causing the hits on target to impact somewhere other than where the shooter intended for them to land. In firearms instructor terminology, this is called "flinching," "jerking" or some other descriptive term, which means the shooter moves the muzzle of the firearm off the target prior to the projectile exiting the barrel.

In blending what firearms professionals know from experience with the academic input of behavioral professionals, we can better understand what is going on in a shooter's mind and body, why this is taking place and, most importantly, how to deal with it so that it is no longer a concern affecting the shooter's ability to hit a target.

A shooter can start the process of controlling the self-preservation response by recognizing a few generally accepted premises.

Humans are innately afraid of unanticipated loud noises because those noises usually signify danger is near. Upon hearing a loud noise — particularly if it is unexpected — an individual tends to experience an involuntarily contracting of muscles and a lowering of the body's center of gravity, preparing to defend against or escape from the perceived danger. A portion of the inner brain, the amygdala, is responsible for this automatic, immediate action.

With proper training and practice, an individual can usually eliminate this errant movement of the muzzle with minimal effort. Success is then achievable.

Humans also have an innate response to protect their eyes by blinking or through physical action. Without vision, protecting oneself from an attack or finding a way to safety is challenging at best. It is common for a human, automatically and without conscious thought, to close his or her eyes when even a small object approaches the face. It is equally as common for an individual's hands to come to the aid of the eyes and push away or deflect any incoming object that the brain perceives as a threat to that individual's vision.

When a shooter is discharging a firearm, there is an involuntary and uncontrollable movement toward that shooter's face at the moment of ignition. The brain senses this as danger to the eyes and triggers an automatic and immediate protective response.

Though this makes sense intellectually, the intellectual or conscious mind's understanding doesn't automatically transfer to the subconscious mind's understanding without some practical programming. It is important that a shooter physically experience a positive, practical exercise along with the intellectual aspect to reprogram the subconscious mind that the noise and the movement of the gun at discharge are of no consequence to his or her personal safety.

Another consideration as to why controlling the self-preservation response is not initially addressed in most shooters' formative training comes from how people learn versus how they are taught to use a firearm.

It is typical for instructors to discuss these factors when they're teaching foundational levels of marksmanship:

- Foot position
- Slightly flexed knees
- Hip position
- Torso position
- Arm position
- Head position
- Dominant-hand position
- Support-hand position
- Grip pressure
- Breath control
- Sight alignment
- Sight picture
- Trigger manipulation

Behavioral professionals tell us that the conscious mind can process, on average, up to seven bits of information simultaneously. Based on my experience, I think three to

five bits of information for the cognitive mind to deal with is more of a realistic average — particularly when a little stress is involved. In either case, the conscious mind has more information than it can handle with all of the pertinent points of performance that a shooter needs to remember, meaning that some get lost in the learning path.

With the conscious mind already overloaded with information, the subconscious mind will not likely recognize the sound and the movement of the firearm at discharge as anything but an attack.

Regular reinforcement of this activity by shooting additional shots removes any likelihood that the shooter will be able to stabilize the muzzle on the target and fire the gun with no effect on that stability. The habit of a flinch is then created and reinforced with each discharge of the firearm. Every time the gun fires, the subconscious mind interprets the noise and recoil as a threat to the shooter's personal safety and takes protective action, closing the eyes and pushing the gun away from the face preemptively.

Once the symptoms are identified, it becomes a relatively simple process to effect a cure.

The shooter needs to understand exactly what the firearm sounds like in the hand at the moment of discharge. This can be accomplished by using a very simple drill that requires the normal shooting and safety equipment and a backstop for the projectiles to impact. The drill will follow the normal guidelines of muzzle management and trigger-finger discipline.

From a typically used shooting position, the shooter should load the gun, point its muzzle at the backstop and then fire it, concentrating only on what the gun sounds like at discharge. The shooter also needs to close his or her eyes to enhance the process (provided the instructor is there to assist in maintaining a safe direction of the muzzle). The shooter should fire as many shots as necessary to understand what the firearm sounds like with each pull of the trigger. It will become apparent that the sound of the gun firing is no threat to the shooter's personal safety. In fact, this exercise will help to show that the sound of the gun firing actually leads to a positive reaction, not a negative one.

This drill usually takes no more than a few shots on average. I've seen it take a magazine or more. I've also seen it take just a few rounds. The shooter should decide when enough is enough in terms of feeling comfortable with the sounds of discharge. Through conscious recognition, the shooter's subconscious is programmed to recognize that the unique sound made by the gun being fired is no longer cause for alarm.

Periodic reinforcement and duplicate drills with each applicable firearm will help, but once the initial exposure is complete, most of the work is done.

The amount of movement of the firearm during recoil is sometimes unknown to a shooter because his or her eyes are shut during discharge. In addition, due to preemptive forward movement applied to the firearm to prevent it from encroaching into the shooter's visual space as the muzzle lifts in recoil, there is little likelihood the shooter will have an accurate awareness of actual gun movement during firing. In either case, the likelihood of the muzzle being pointed at the target when the projectile exits is low.

Another simple drill requiring safety and shooting gear, along with a safe backstop, will condition the subconscious to no longer react adversely to the movement of the firearm during discharge and recoil.

The shooter will assume a normal shooting position, pointing the loaded firearm into the backstop. The individual will then move his or her head to

MARKSMANSHIP SIMPLIFIED | www.USConcealedCarry.com | 41

the inside of the shooting position in order to clearly see the muzzle and the side of the firearm when discharge occurs. After firing several shots to determine the actual range of movement of the gun during discharge, the shooter should reposition the head to the outside of the shooting position, allowing observation of the opposite side of the firearm during discharge. The shooter will fire the final shots with both head and eyes directly behind the firearm, focusing on something closer to the face than the sights, such as the hammer or the rear of the slide. Once the shooter realizes the actual minimal movement of the firearm rather than the perceived movement, it will be much easier to overcome the temptation of actively resisting the firearm's movement at discharge.

Controlling the self-preservation response is a simple matter once a shooter understands the core reasons for the involuntary movement. Simple self-checks should accompany each shooting session to verify that errant movement is not allowed to affect the muzzle's relationship to the target during firing. Being aware of the blast signature at the muzzle during discharge confirms that a shooter's visual attention is where it should be for precision shot delivery. Noticing spent shells or cartridge cases in the ejection process when a shooter is firing a semi-automatic gives similar input. Watching the smooth vertical rise and fall of the muzzle in relation to the target is another visual indicator that verifies good shooting techniques.

Shooting is simple. All that a shooter has to do to hit the target is stabilize the muzzle on the target and cause discharge with no change in that stability.

Once this foundational platform of marksmanship is in place, the shooter will quickly advance in tactical skills training. Simplicity leads to success — particularly if the instructor removes the obstacles to learning rather than overloading students with too much information.

CONSCIOUS MIND

The cognitive mind, also referred to as the "thinking mind" or the "conscious mind," is where the initial stages of learning take place.

Cognitive learning is the acquisition of knowledge and skill through experience and the senses. The senses of feeling, seeing and hearing are prevalent in marksmanship and shooting. The information, the goals and the objectives are disseminated from the instructor to students by explanation and demonstration prior to replication.

Ultimately, much of the information presented to students will be cognitively processed and downloaded into their subconscious minds for permanent storage and immediate recall when needed.

The most effective means of communicating marksmanship to the cognitive mind is to present material in the simplest manner possible — and that means indisputable and easy to replicate. Information presented in this way leaves little need for question and analysis before being accepted by students as valid and rendered into permanent storage.

The conscious (cognitive, thinking) mind is the "gatekeeper" of information that is to be permanently retained in the subconscious mind.

For information to pass through the conduit from the conscious to the subconscious mind for future use, it first must pass a battery of tests.

These tests vary somewhat from person to person but serve to validate the information or action as being beneficial to an individual.

Some key elements for passage through the "gate" might include how relevant and realistic the information is to the recipient. Does the information make sense? Does it compare to information previously learned? Is it believable? Can it be reproduced in a reasonably short timespan? Why is it important to the shooter? What's its priority in everyday life?

If the material presented is considered indisputable by the recipient, the likelihood of immediate acceptance and direct download into permanent storage for future use is near 100 percent.

The cognitive mind is perpetually bombarded with information from all of the senses. The number of bits of information that can be processed decreases as emotions, including fear, increase in prevalence. Under grave circumstances, the information processed by the cognitive mind decreases to an insignificant level.

Information previously processed, recognized as valuable and downloaded into the long-term memory of the subconscious mind takes over once the cognitive mind is overwhelmed.

For this reason, it's vital that any information pertaining to marksmanship — the ability to hit a target on demand — be simple, believable, quickly achievable and repeatable and be accepted and passed into the subconscious mind by the cognitive mind.

SUBCONSCIOUS MIND

The subconscious mind is the portion of the brain that runs automatically in the background without focus or thought. It comes preprogrammed at birth with a large number of self-preservation responses to protect the body from harm. It drives eye-hand coordination, which allows someone to point a finger at anything that's been visually identified as an object of interest. It also maintains automatic functions of the body necessary for life, such as blood flow and breathing. Emotions such as joy, sorrow, pleasure and fear are all products of the subconscious mind. A vast number of memories, originating from life's experiences and available for reference, are stored there. The subconscious mind can be trained to respond to specific stimuli, performing an act or action on cue in the most consistent and perfect manner possible, when it's programmed to run autonomously. Subconscious action is much faster and more efficient than action generated by conscious thought, and it typically produces a more desirable result. How the subconscious mind is used and controlled can be the difference between success and failure in the broad scope of marksmanship. In the areas of precision shooting, speed shooting or a combination of both, a shooter learning and downloading what it takes to hit a specific target consistently will train the eyes and the hands to work together with the brain to deliver a shot with the utmost of precision and timing.

This involves mastering the visual, physical and mental mechanics necessary to deliver acceptably accurate shots. Repetition of these mechanics helps to fine-tune them, resulting in consistency and repeatability. Ultimately, the subconscious records all of the necessary physical, visual and mental requirements for performing the task and stores the information for recall when needed. Ideally, this programming is refined and reinforced regularly to maintain the highest level of performance.

Information that is simple, makes sense and is relatively easy to replicate has the highest likelihood of quickly entering someone's subconscious mind and being recalled by the individual on demand.

Consistency in shot delivery is essential for the highest level of performance in marksmanship. Consistency is best realized by formulating a plan for each shot. This, when combined with the right equipment, yields maximum performance within a shooter's physical capabilities.

"The plan" is a series of cues, words, phrases or thoughts that help a shooter initiate, deliver and finish the shot. In simplified learning, three steps in the process are most effective for the average shooter (because of the "A, B, C" or "1, 2, 3" method used in the formative stages of learning as a child).

An example could be the words "target," "sights" and "trigger."

The actions to follow each word might be described in the following way:

- *Target* means to find the target to be engaged.
- *Sights* means to superimpose the sights on the target, establishing the proper sight picture and eye focus.
- Trigger means moving the trigger rearward until recoil takes place.

The speed with which this happens can be as fast or as slow as the shooter needs to shoot or is capable of shooting.

Another example might be as simple as "see a target" immediately followed by "shoot it." What this means to

the shooter is that once a target has been identified, getting the muzzle on target and then pulling the trigger are the next steps for success.

To get to either of these levels, a shooter has to learn the foundational skills, fine-tune them to an acceptable level and program them into the subconscious mind for future use. Practice of these skills individually or collectively provides the subconscious with memory inventory from which to draw when the need arises.

Having a proven plan that works, regardless of the subject matter, instills confidence in an individual's ability to perform. If a shooter knows what needs to happen and has performed certain actions previously under similar circumstances multiple times, there is no doubt that he or she can repeat that same effort as many times as desired or required.

Anyone who has participated in a competitive shooting event has experienced something called "match pressure." This can be defined as performance anxiety or fear of failure. These negative emotions come from the subconscious and are the nemesis of many who compete in any discipline, including shooting. Any question over which the shooter has no control, such as another shooter's score or a change in the weather, starts to cloud the conscious mind. It creates self-doubt and distracts the shooter from focusing on "the plan" and performing to the level of his or her capability.

Having confidence in the plan and the fortitude to follow it helps to suppress the negative thoughts that enter a shooter's mind. Visualization — a means of mentally rehearsing the execution of the predetermined plan with the desired results — will keep the mind focused on the job at hand. Self-talk that is reasonable and makes sense is another method to overcome the "what ifs" and "if onlys" that sometime plague a competitor. The knowledge that prior preparation equals performance will help in combating negative thinking. A shooter's expectation should be to shoot at a personal best level (with the knowledge and acceptance that it doesn't always end that way).

Attitude has much to do with how the subconscious affects personal performance. Someone who keeps a positive attitude and stays focused on the job at hand will usually outperform the negative thinker who is a habitual complainer.

The ultimate goal for the firearms practitioner, whether it be for competition or combat, is to find the ability to be "in the zone" while operating the tools of the trade. While this may have multiple meanings, the end result is the same: to perform exceptionally under a variety of circumstances. Being "in the zone" refers to what some regard as an "out-of-body experience." In truth, it is subconsciously performing with no influence from the conscious mind. It's like being on autopilot, effortlessly acting and reacting to outside stimuli without having to employ conscious thought. In fact, if the conscious mind is allowed to participate in the performance, the results are slowed and diminished.

Any top-level shooter spends a lot of time and effort understanding the what, why and how of the techniques of a particular discipline as well as perfecting those techniques to maximize effectiveness and efficiency. Through practice and repetition, this knowledge and ability is downloaded and stored in the subconscious as a response to certain cues. The shooter's confidence in his or her ability to perform on cue delivers the subconscious response when the stimulus to respond presents itself.

Relaxation — the ability to calm the mind and body under pressure — is essential to maximizing performance. Experience, recognized ability, a proven plan, visualization of perfect performance, positive self-talk, a positive attitude and the ability to ignore concerns beyond one's control all contribute to mind and body relaxation, which leads to being in the zone.

Those who are more technically proficient, confident in their plans and in control of their mental attributes are far more likely to achieve that level of success than others.

OODA LOOP

The OODA Loop is an acronym for "observe, orient, decide and act." It's a four-step process developed for combat but derived from how people make daily decisions. It is a fluid blend of the conscious and subconscious minds working in tandem to problem-solve the challenges that individuals must face. With experience and training, the subconscious mind takes on more of the decision-making responsibility, therefore streamlining the amount of time necessary to come to a decision. This is particularly important in critical-incident thinking involving personal defense, combat and life-or-death situations.

In an effort to explain the facets of decision-making in aerial combat, U.S. Air Force Col. John Boyd developed the OODA Loop after his tour in the Korean War. It is said that Col. Boyd could neutralize an adversary in 40 seconds or less from initial observation to destruction in aerial combat, validating the concept.

As previously stated, the OODA Loop is a description of how people make decisions every day. How and what they learn as they are exposed to more information that is relevant to the conditions at hand tends to speed up the decision process — so much so that there may be little to no conscious thought involved in acting on a stimulus (what is referred to as an "observation"). One of the ideas regarding the OODA Loop in combat is increasing the speed in which the action is generated. Simply said, an individual faster into action than an opponent has the upper hand and a higher probability of winning the contest.

Studying each of the four stages of the OODA Loop with a broader viewpoint will help break down the concept and how it is used in a variety of situations in everyday life.

The observation stage means gathering information with all of the senses — including the sixth, intuition — rather than only the sense of sight. A person alert to the world is constantly receiving input from all of the senses. Much of it is discarded automatically as being irrelevant. However, when an individual perceives a condition that may be dangerous, he or she naturally orients attention in that direction. This doesn't necessarily mean facing the condition physically but rather giving it full attention in order to respond to it effectively.

The orient stage is believed to be the most critical of the four stages since it is where a person analyzes the input of the observation and then decides what to do (or bypasses deciding). An individual can move directly to action if previous training, experiences and

Photo courtesy of Marine Corps History Division, Archives Branch

beliefs are strongly ingrained in the subconscious mind. In other words, the individual goes directly to action without conscious thought. This eliminates going through the decision phase of the OODA Loop, which saves time.

Sometimes an individual has previous experience or training related to the observed condition. The more this training and experience have been repeated and reinforced, the quicker that individual's brain will make the comparison and act subconsciously. This subconscious processing shortens the response time (action) in countering or defeating an adversary, allowing the defender to respond to a threat before the threat has time to respond. It's not hard to understand that the person who strikes first usually has the upper hand.

90/10

The important thing to remember is that subconscious thought is infinitely faster than conscious thought. In general, using conscious thought takes approximately 1/4 second for each of the four steps of the OODA Loop or one whole second to process and act on the observed information. Subconscious action can be virtually instantaneous. As an example, when touching a hot object, an individual doesn't have to think through the process of removing his or her hand from the object. The individual responds automatically and instantly. In this case, pain immediately creates action.

Repeated, realistic training relevant to a specific subject or situation conditions an individual to subconsciously respond faster than an adversary.

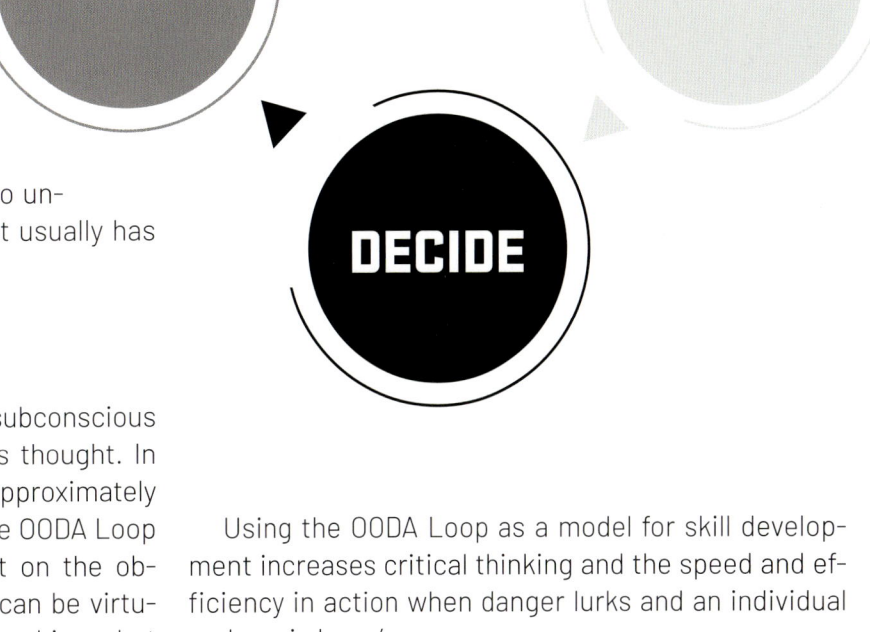

Using the OODA Loop as a model for skill development increases critical thinking and the speed and efficiency in action when danger lurks and an individual ends up in harm's way.

When compared to the mechanical aspects of marksmanship, the mental aspects cover a much greater range of territory. Few will disagree that shooting is 90 percent mental. Unfortunately, many people consider the mental aspects of marksmanship only after all other pursuits for success have failed to deliver the desired results.

CHAPTER 6
VISUAL FACTORS

Human vision is said to be a person's pathway to the world. Those in academia suggest that as much as 80 percent of the information that is received by the brain enters through an individual's eyes. Yet a person rarely uses this sense of sight to its full capabilities.

Much of this comes from lack of need. Some comes from lack of recognition of how vision is subconsciously used. And some comes from lack of education and training. All of these factors feed into complacency until a reason to cultivate the most prevalent sense arises. The study of human vision and how the eyes work can enhance life. For many people, there is a whole new world right in front of them that they never noticed. The phrase "looking but not seeing" becomes a little more defined in its meaning.

For a shooter, target discrimination can be a challenge — especially as it relates to hunting, personal defense or combat situations. Once a shooter has located a target, the next challenge is how to best use the attributes of vision to hit the target with the firearm in hand. In addition, the shooter must factor in these considerations:

- Distance to the target
- Size of the target
- Light conditions
- Type of gun and sights on the gun
- Environmental conditions
- Location
- Movement
- Available time

When factoring in these and perhaps other considerations not mentioned, it becomes apparent that a shooter's eyes play a paramount role in achieving success.

It is important to understand, from a layman's point of view, what the capabilities of human vision are and how the eye works. Keep in mind that every eye is different and that there are plenty of variables with which to contend. Nearsightedness, farsightedness and astigmatism, or a combination of one or more of these, pose challenges to a shooter. Eye dominance can also be troublesome to a shooter. Fortunately, a shooter can work through these variables by following a few simple guidelines.

Conventional training presents some concepts and misconceptions regarding marksmanship and what is necessary to see in order to hit a target. Many of these come as absolutes, without deviation, but in reality they don't provide a full picture of how someone can be a successful shooter. What comes next will enlighten and provide a shooter with an understanding of how to better utilize human vision with whatever equipment is available — with or without optical aids.

IRON SIGHTS

Handguns equipped with a front sight and a rear sight are referred to as having "iron sights," although they may be made of different materials. These sights may be fixed, drift-adjustable for windage, or fully adjustable for windage and elevation. The manner in which they are used to guide a bullet to a target is the same. The more adjustments available, the more latitude a shooter has in ammunition types and sight-picture options.

Sight alignment on a handgun with a front and rear sight requires visually centering — both vertically and horizontally — the front sight in the rear-sight notch. Typically, a shooter will verify the amount of light

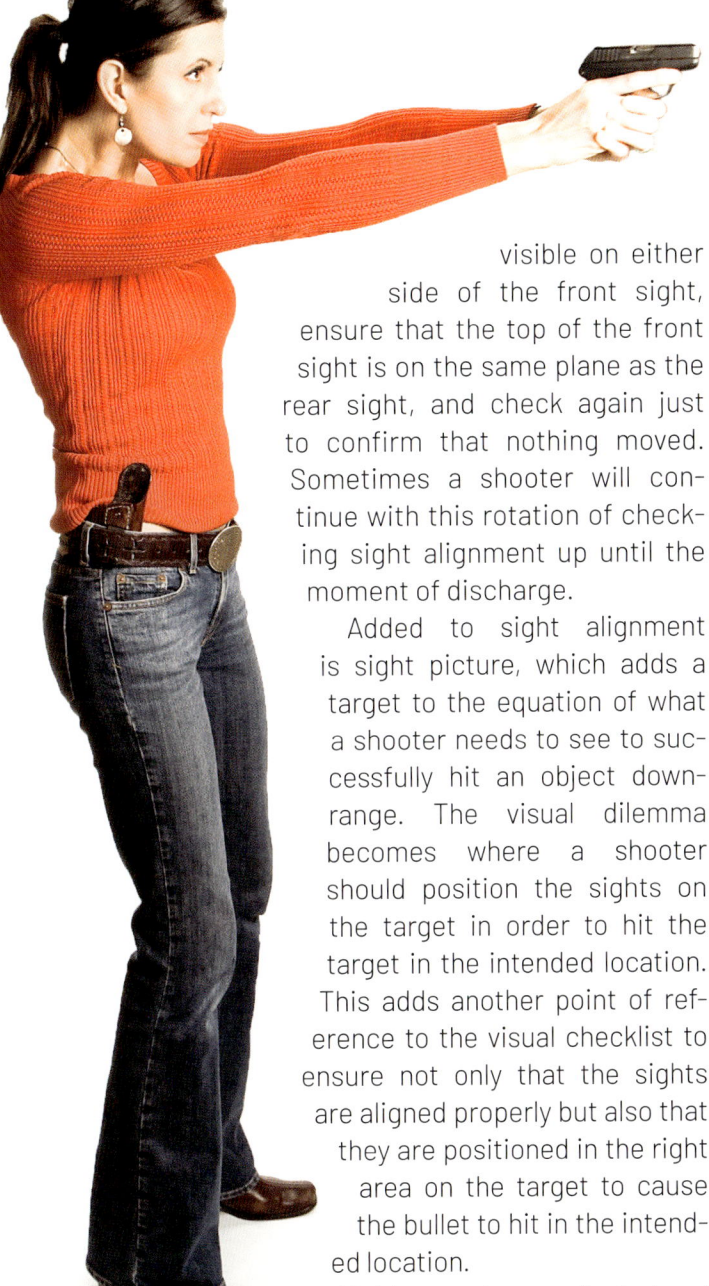

There is an easy way to establish and maintain sight alignment and sight picture — making this concept simple and understandable — and that's by learning about and using the natural capabilities of human vision.

The eye can easily and accurately find and see the center of an object or combination of objects. When a shooter is viewing the front sight through the rear-sight opening, the front sight will automatically center itself. If the front sight has a round dot, fiber optic or night sight embedded in it, it is even easier for the shooter to see the dot centered in the window created by the rear-sight opening because of the contrasting color and shape. The smaller size and round shape of the dot makes it easier for the eye to focus on the front sight through the rear-sight opening, resulting in automatic alignment.

When a target is introduced to the equation, the eye automatically identifies the center of the target, regardless of shape or size.

Assuming the gun is zeroed to "point of aim equals point of impact," all a shooter has to do is see the dot in the front sight through the rear-sight opening, centered on the target, to hit the target in the center of mass.

Using the eye's natural centering ability aligns the sights and provides an easily attainable sight picture, providing accuracy and consistency shot after shot.

There is another benefit to using this method of achieving the proper sight alignment and sight picture. Those shooters who wear prescription glasses or who find it difficult to see the sights as well as they once did will discover a significant improvement in their shooting performance by using this sighting technique.

And for those shooters who don't see the sights as sharply and as clearly as they would like, there is a perspective worth noting that may prove beneficial in

visible on either side of the front sight, ensure that the top of the front sight is on the same plane as the rear sight, and check again just to confirm that nothing moved. Sometimes a shooter will continue with this rotation of checking sight alignment up until the moment of discharge.

Added to sight alignment is sight picture, which adds a target to the equation of what a shooter needs to see to successfully hit an object downrange. The visual dilemma becomes where a shooter should position the sights on the target in order to hit the target in the intended location. This adds another point of reference to the visual checklist to ensure not only that the sights are aligned properly but also that they are positioned in the right area on the target to cause the bullet to hit in the intended location.

If this sounds complicated and busy, it is! Unnecessarily so.

maintaining a high level of marksmanship for as long as they are actively shooting.

The words "reference" and "contrast" take on new meanings pertaining to being able to hit a target — any target.

"Reference" in this context means something on which to put the sights. In other words, it is something at which to aim, such as a target.

"Contrast" in this context means being able to distinguish the difference between the front sight, the rear sight and the target. Contrary to conventional thinking, so long as a shooter can see the front sight and the rear sight as two different objects and can align those sights relative to a target sufficiently to hit the target, the sights do not have to be perfectly clear in order to get the hit.

A shooter who is in the fourth or fifth decade of life might find it much more difficult to see the sights on a pistol as clearly as in the past. The edges of the front and rear sights are blurred and sometimes appear to merge with one another, making it difficult for a shooter to distinguish one from the other while trying to establish alignment.

An easy way to solve this problem is to widen the rear-sight notch enough so that the blurry front sight and the blurry rear-sight notch can be distinguished from one another. The eye will automatically center the front sight in the rear-sight opening to align the sights. Superimposing the aligned blurry sight set over the center of the target, again allowing the eye to naturally find the center of the target, will produce amazing results.

An effective alternative to widening the rear-sight notch is to paint the rear portion of the sights — where a shooter observes them — contrasting colors so that they can be individually distinguished for alignment. The concept of letting the eye center the front sight in the rear-sight opening and centering that combination where the bullets are intended to impact is the same in either case.

Letting the eyes naturally do the work necessary to hit a target improves the rate of success and saves time and frustration when a shooter is practicing marksmanship.

MINI RED-DOT SIGHTS

A pistol equipped with a mini red-dot sight (MRDS) features an alternative or additional sighting system to the standard post-and-notch iron sights found on most handguns. The MRDS is designed to benefit the shooter with a method of sighting, which in many cases delivers a speed and accuracy advantage over conventional iron sights. An MRDS can be used as a stand-alone sight system for competition or sport shooting or in tandem with iron sights, which is recommended for the personal-defense shooter as a backup in case of electronic failure.

The fact that there is only the red dot to align with the target for an acceptable sight picture simplifies the aiming process of an MRDS over conventional iron sights.

A consideration when adding a mini red-dot sight to an existing pistol or transitioning to a pistol that's equipped with an MRDS is how the gun's iron sights are configured.

It is essential that the personal-defense pistol have backup iron sights that co-witness with the red dot in the MRDS. This provides a safety net for the shooter in case the MRDS fails the moment it is needed.

Another benefit to having co-witnessed backup iron sights is that they assist the shooter in the initial stages of training in the use of and familiarization with the MRDS. Initially, the iron sights assist the transitioning shooter in visually obtaining dot-on-target acquisition when he or she draws from the holster.

A common complaint for many new to an MRDS is that the red dot is always in the top of the screen or even higher when they draw to shoot a target.

There are two simple ways to overcome this deficiency, and they can be combined or used independently.

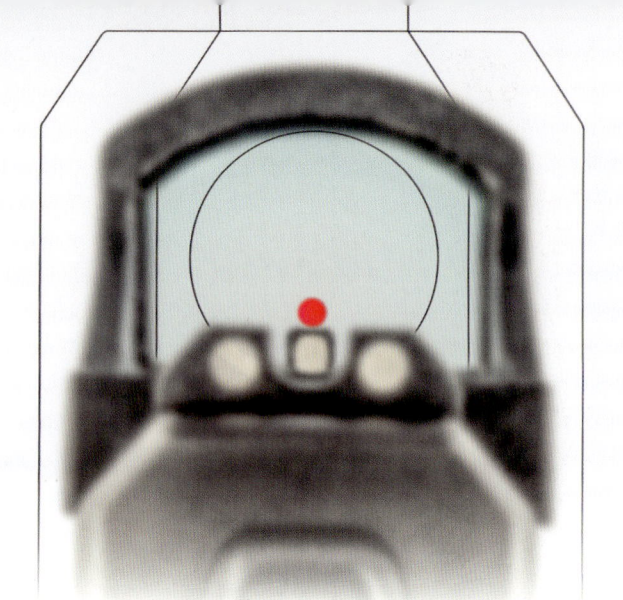 

The first is primarily visual in nature. By using the backup iron sights as a reference in getting the muzzle on the target as previously practiced, a shooter will find that the co-witnessed red dot comes into view during the draw and presentation to the target. This makes it easier for the shooter to visually pick up the dot and get it on the target during the trigger pull. With minimal practice on the shooter's part, the primary focus of the eye will transition from the iron sights to the red dot, leaving the iron sights as a secondary point of reference in the visual field.

The second method is more of a tactile execution of spatial awareness. This is accomplished by practicing the draw to the target slowly enough to experience the "feel" (position) of the arms and hands in relation to the eyes necessary to get the dot on the target in the most direct manner. Doing this dry at first is beneficial because it isolates the action to only what is visually necessary to accomplish the task of getting the dot on the target. Therefore, a shooter is conditioning the body to respond naturally and automatically to getting the gun on target expediently. After satisfactory dry work, the shooter can perform live-fire to validate the process. In many cases, this improves a shooter's skill level just by fine-tuning — with smoothness and efficiency — the previously practiced draw and presentation.

One distinct advantage to an MRDS is that it allows the shooter to look at the target as the dot is superimposed over the impact area to deliver accurate hits. If the shooter sees the dot on the target, whether focus is on the dot or the target, hits will occur.

To be candid, there are two schools of thought as to where the eye should be focused when a shooter is aiming with an MRDS, and both have merit.

One is to focus intently on the dot — just as a shooter would the front sight of an iron-sight-equipped pistol. This makes it easy for the iron-sight shooter to transition to an MRDS and back again without having to change focal points.

In either case, the target is out of focus, and holding center gives the best results.

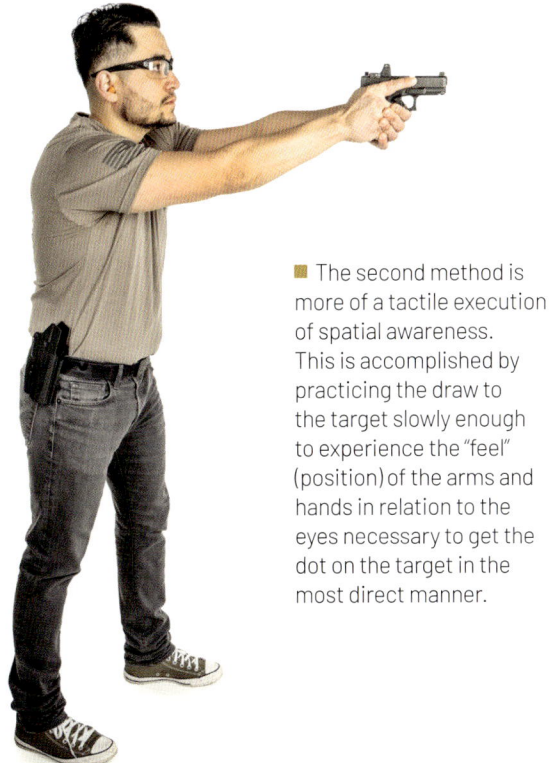

■ The second method is more of a tactile execution of spatial awareness. This is accomplished by practicing the draw to the target slowly enough to experience the "feel" (position) of the arms and hands in relation to the eyes necessary to get the dot on the target in the most direct manner.

The other perspective is for the shooter to focus intently on the part of the target that needs to be hit and allow the out-of-focus dot to hover over that area.

From a tactical perspective, focusing on the desired point of impact while superimposing the red dot on that area as the shooter pulls the trigger makes a lot of sense, all things considered.

My suggestion is to try both and favor the one that results in the desired performance.

An additional feature of an MRDS is the variability of size and brightness of the actual dot. Brightness corresponds with size; the brighter the dot, the bigger the dot appears. Ambient light conditions set the baseline as to how bright the dot setting needs to be. This may vary depending on how and where the MRDS is being used. In bright, outdoor conditions, the dot needs to be set at a higher level in order for the shooter to pick it up visually with ease. In low-light conditions, the dot brightness and size requirement are at a lower level. With practice and experience, a shooter will find what level of brightness aids in the best shots and thus the best performance.

EYE DOMINANCE

One of the first things to do when learning to become a good marksman is to establish eye dominance. The dominant eye is the one the body has chosen to give primary input to the brain. Ideally, the dominant eye corresponds with the dominant hand. Unfortunately, there is a sizable portion of the population whose dominant hands and dominant eyes are opposites.

These individuals are referred to as "cross-dominant" shooters.

An easy way to determine eye dominance is to have a shooter extend the dominant-side arm and make a circle with the thumb and index finger. Then, have the individual view a small object, such as a light switch on the wall, through the circle. While focusing on the object, the shooter should close or occlude one eye and then the other. The eye that remains focused on the object when the other eye is closed or occluded is the shooter's dominant eye.

Few realize that eye dominance is a variable that can change in an instant. This depends on the strength of the dominance, physical condition and other related factors. In fact, there are people who are co-dominant; whose eyes are so evenly matched that neither takes precedence over the other.

It is best for the novice pistol shooter to start with a gun in the hand that corresponds to the dominant eye.

If this is not possible, there are several remedies that can help to overcome this problem. These remedies will vary with both the application and the firearm the shooter is using.

Even a seasoned shooter who is struggling with difficulties regarding seeing the sights consistently can use these remedies to elevate performance.

The shooter should keep both eyes open when sighting a pistol, if possible. This reduces eye strain and maximizes the visual input to the brain.

The simplest and most versatile way for the cross-dominant shooter to attain optimal sight alignment and sight picture is to turn the head slightly — allowing the dominant eye to take precedence over the other — while keeping both eyes open.

An alternative method of sighting is to have a shooter partially squint the dominant eye, limiting the amount of light and visual information being transmitted to the brain. This forces the shooter's other eye to take precedence in seeing and controlling the shot. This method works well in the short term; however, prolonged use will result in eye fatigue, which can degrade overall shooting performance.

A target shooter shooting at a static target has the option of occluding the dominant eye, which blocks the visual image but still allows ambient light to enter the eye. This can be accomplished by placing an opaque covering on or in front of the lens of the shooting glasses. A word of caution: Do not use an eye patch to cover the eye since this restricts the light from entering the eye and will result in eye fatigue for both eyes. It is important that both eyes have the availability of similar amounts of light to function at their best even though visual imagery and information may be restricted to a single eye.

CENTRAL VISION

The following factors pertaining to the characteristics of central vision are valuable to a shooter in that they help with understanding how to best use the natural attributes of the eye to maximize performance.

A heavy concentration of light receptors in the eye's retina — referred to as "cones" — are responsible for an individual's central vision. Central vision is the foundation of visual information for humans — and especially a shooter. It can be described as a narrow field of input (about 2 to 5 degrees) to the eye that allows a shooter to see shapes, sharp images and colors and that locks on to anything that has attracted his or her visual attention.

Central vision can find the center of an object through observation regardless of the object's shape or size. Focus length for optimal clarity of an object being observed is approximately 5 to 6 inches. Any objects outside of that small window are visible but out of focus to varying degrees.

With the combined input from both eyes, central vision provides depth perception and target discrimination to as little as 1 minute of angle (MOA), which is 1.047 inches at 100 yards. Central vision is saccadic, which means that it maintains a specific point of reference — visual attention — for only a short period of time before it identifies and locks on to a different point of reference.

Visual attention can be controlled through training the conscious or subconscious mind. A shooter can look at, but not see, an object without a cue from the brain telling the eye specifically what it is supposed to see. The amount of light entering (and information observed by) the eye is immeasurable. Only portions of that information are processed and used — based on the needs of the shooter — at any given time.

It is important that a shooter and marksman understand and cultivate, through training, the capabilities of the eye's central vision and then download these capabilities into subconscious action for future use. As an example, when a shooter is aiming an iron-sight pistol for a precision shot, the eye should be intensely focused on the smallest identifiable spot on the face of the front sight — the very center of a night sight or a single serration of a serrated ramp, for instance.

Although it's not as well-defined as the front sight, the rear sight is visible in the 6- to 8-degree field of a shooter's paracentral, or near-peripheral, vision, as the two sights are aligned automatically by a shooter's eye.

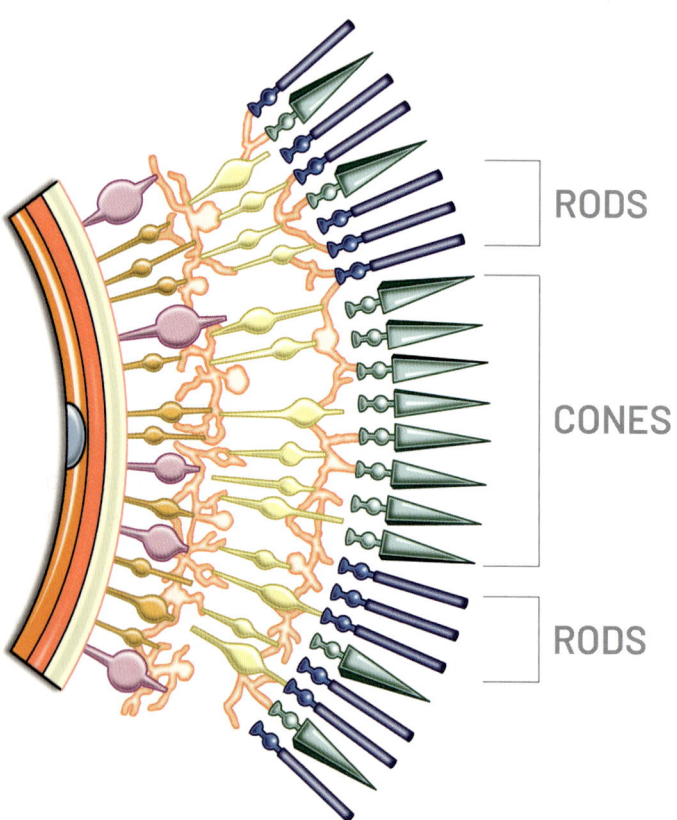

The target, even though out of focus, has its center automatically defined by the eye's discrimination capabilities.

Marksmanship skills can be cultivated and committed to subconscious action, requiring minimal time and effort on a shooter's part, by using the eye's natural capabilities of centering the front sight in the rear-sight opening for proper alignment and by holding the aligned sights on the accurately perceived center of the target. With sufficient repetition, this process, combined with good trigger control, will become an automatic response of successfully hitting a target when the proper cues are given.

PERIPHERAL VISION

The following factors pertaining to the characteristics of peripheral vision are valuable to a shooter. They help a shooter understand how to best use the natural attributes of the eye to maximize marksmanship performance.

Peripheral vision can be described as the visual input that occurs outside of the central point of attention (referred to as "central vision"). Peripheral vision is controlled by light receptors (called "rods") located over most of the eye's retina. Rods work to complement the cones in the eye with information that is often ignored by the brain unless specifically categorized

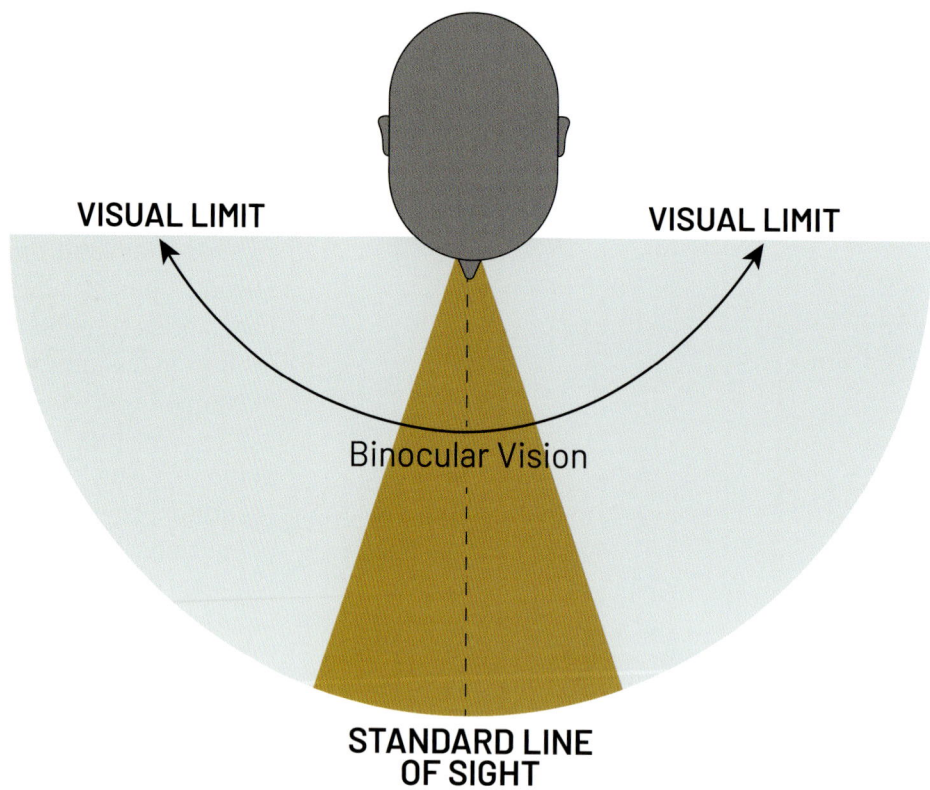

as important. Even though rods provide secondary input to the brain, they become primary in low-light conditions when the cones of central vision shut down due to lack of stimulation. At that point, object color becomes unavailable and only gray scales register as visual input. When vision is reduced to gray scales — considered "low-light vision" — total visual input is as much as 30 times less than when the eye can distinguish color.

The average individual's peripheral vision is limited vertically and horizontally by the placement and position of the eyes in the head. The nose, cheeks and forehead obstruct information input to varying degrees, but most people are able to receive information input to 180 degrees or greater when both eyes are used simultaneously.

Peripheral vision is hardly given a thought, much less cultivated and used intentionally. A person who walks without tripping and falling, for example, is successfully using peripheral vision without really thinking about it.

For the shooter and marksman, a practical understanding of the benefits of peripheral vision can be of great value — especially in a combat or personal-defense context. Awareness of movement, for instance, is a helpful characteristic of peripheral vision that aids in target detection and identification. Indeed, being peripherally aware of danger or unforeseen obstacles in the environment improves target detection. And eye-hand coordination functions well peripherally, enabling justifiable target engagement with efficiency and accuracy.

Peripheral vision can be practiced and improved with minimal effort if an individual is consciously aware of his or her surroundings in daily activities. This conscious awareness becomes a subconscious habit, and life itself takes on new meaning through a more complete awareness of one's surroundings.

OPTIMIZING SKILLS

Understanding how the eye functions and how to best utilize those functions will go a long way toward optimizing a marksman's shooting skills. Learning what one needs to see to produce a consistently good shot under a variety of conditions is the making of a well-rounded shooter.

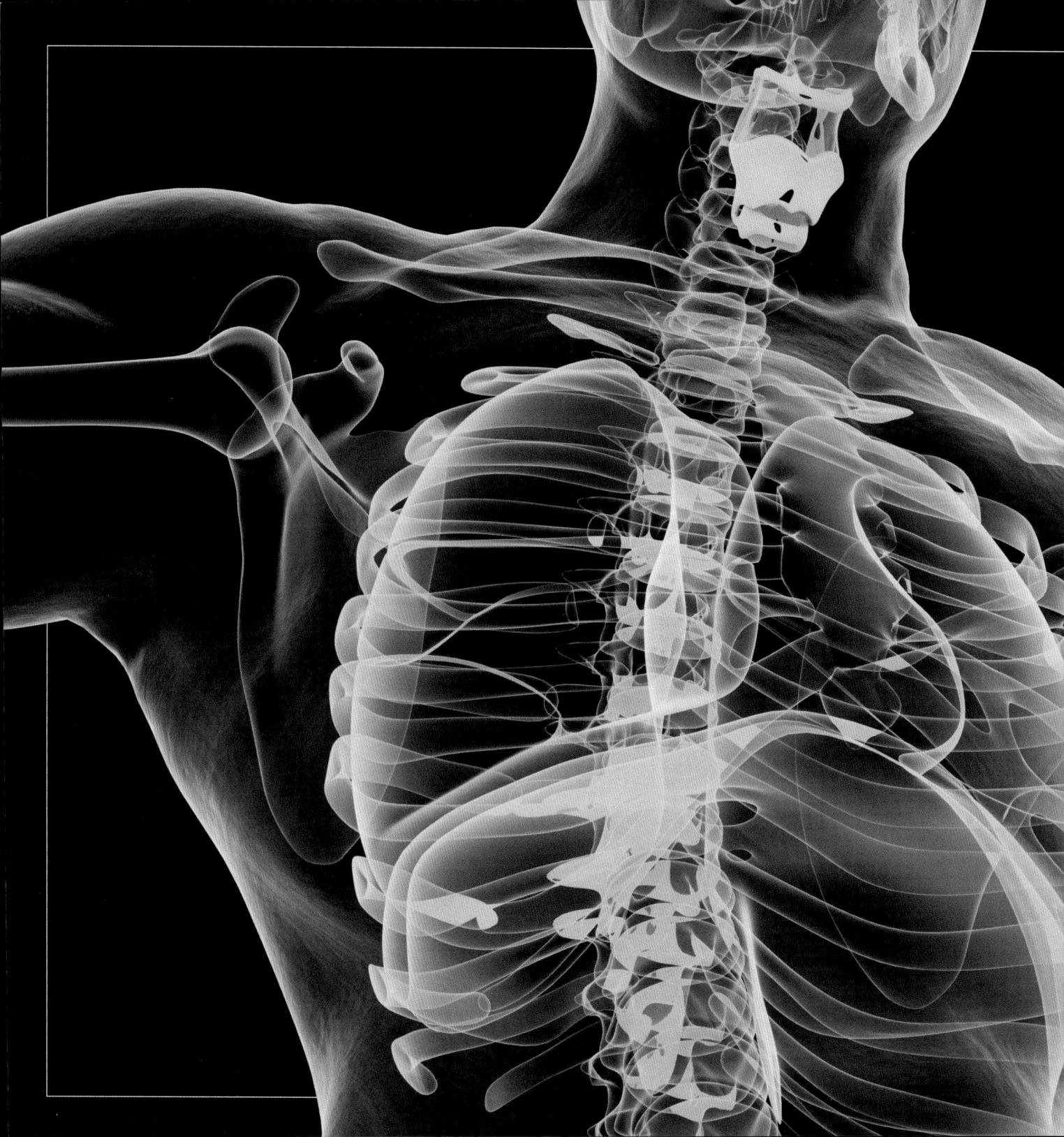

CHAPTER 7
BIOMECHANICAL FACTORS

The study of biomechanical factors from the perspective of pistol marksmanship can be described as how the body's skeletal and muscular systems move and work together while an individual is interacting with a handgun.

A shooter's goal is to maximize performance with improved technique, economy of motion and simplicity of execution — all without compromising safety or incurring injury.

DIFFERENT SHAPES AND SIZES

Human physiology experts divide humans into three different somatotypes (body shapes or physiques):
- Ectomorphs (slim and slightly built)
- Mesomorphs (muscular and fit)
- Endomorphs (rounder and heavier)

They further separate these three categories into subsets.

Every person is biomechanically different, and when age, health and fitness level are taken into consideration, it becomes readily apparent that there is no one-size-fits-all solution to achieving the best shooting results.

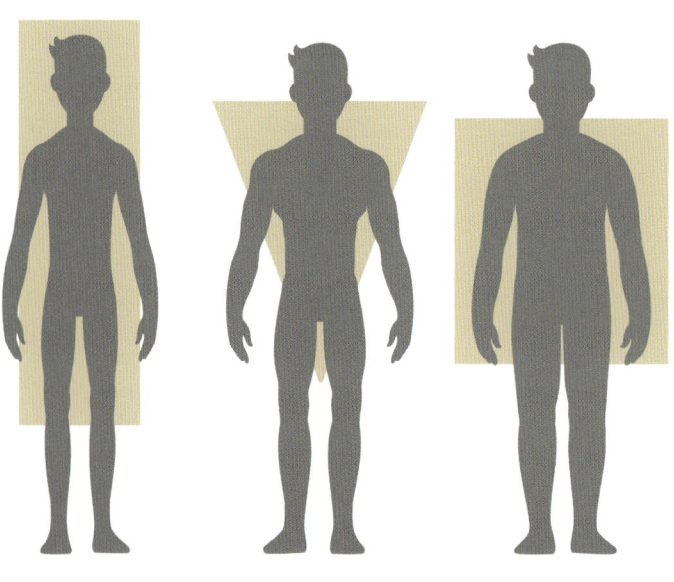

ECTOMORPH   MESOMORPH   ENDOMORPH

EMPLOYING NATURAL ATTRIBUTES

While there may be some general guidelines for shooting positions and techniques, instructors and students should always identify and take advantage of their natural attributes to accomplish the best results. This is where objective-based training enters into the discussion.

When it comes to a skill-building scenario, a good place to start is to ask what the shooter wishes to accomplish with the exercise, followed by why it is important for the shooter to know and perform

the skill. An instructor must be able to demonstrate and explain the "how" to students and follow up with practical application that provides each student with the latitude to accomplish the "what" through whatever physical movement is personally easiest.

Consider how a shooter develops a combat shooting stance. The "what" is for the shooter to develop a stationary position capable of sufficient muzzle stability on the target and to hit the target with as many shots as necessary to neutralize the threat before moving or engaging other targets. When it comes to the "why" in a combat situation, the shooter's survival is dependent on accomplishing the "what" in the most efficient way and within the available time and resources. The "how" does not need to be a whole litany of foot, arm, hand and head descriptions and positionings; instead, it should include a brief description of what the shooter needs to do using actions previously learned in other aspects of life.

BUILDING FUNDAMENTALS
Body Position

To accomplish the "what," the shooter, while standing, must find a position of balance that enables stabilizing the muzzle on the target for more than one shot and that allows smooth movement out of the position (to an improved one), if necessary. Does it really matter what position the shooter's feet are in or what percentage of weight is on the balls of the feet? What about any other factors that must be taken into consideration for a shooter to accomplish the "what"?

Humans have different centers of gravity, ranges of motion, flexibility and mobility. Some also have injuries or afflictions that can interfere with the textbook methods of how to get into one of the three or more recommended shooting stances.

Keep in mind that combat and some types of competitive shooting have parallels (namely, the speed and efficiency with which shots must be delivered). Therefore, many training techniques are similar. When a shooter's primary concern is precision shot placement on a target, the "what" shifts to maintaining balance with maximum stability of the muzzle on the target for consistent delivery over multiple shots. The "how" is using bone support and muscle relaxation to find natural point of aim, which will in turn maximize muzzle stability on the target. Bone support is using the skeletal system to maintain a consistent body position relative to the target, with minimal muscle tension used to sustain that position. Natural point of aim is little more than holding the gun in the shooting position with a minimal amount of muscle tension. After attaining this neutral position of muzzle stability, a shooter can move his or her feet to help position the muzzle on the center of the target.

The objective is for the muzzle to position itself on the center of the target each time the shooter raises the gun to shoot that target. The natural point of aim will change as the body settles and the muscles relax. This happens differently with each individual, making it prudent to check natural point of aim periodically and adjust as necessary to stabilize the muzzle in the middle of the target.

Grip

Grip is a shooter's foundation for controlling a pistol. There are many discussions in the firearms community about a one-handed versus two-handed grip, a strong-hand versus support-hand grip, how much pressure to apply with either hand, and so on. All of these suggestions either come from someone's personal experience or are a regurgitation of what that individual has heard from someone else. However, it is easy to overlook how this information applies to the person learning how to grip a pistol. Given that hand size, hand strength, range of motion and physical condition all impact how a person holds a pistol, there are too many variables to be able to settle on one definitive method of gripping a gun.

Grip can be broken down into several segments of achieving the best performance under a given set of circumstances.

For the best results, the pistol needs to fit the shooter's hand. In this regard, the two main concerns are size — specifically the circumference of the grip — and trigger reach, which is the distance a shooter's trigger finger must extend to pull the trigger.

The objective is to fit the gun to the palm of the hand so that the barrel points to the same location on the target as where the extended index finger points. Equally important are the shooter's ability to reach the trigger and to maintain sufficient contact with the trigger in order to pull it parallel to the gun's frame, multiple times and with little to no lateral pressure, which could move the muzzle off target.

This is a simple and easy starting point that a shooter can accomplish in a few moments. Start by selecting an unloaded pistol with which the shooter can work. With the slide forward and the trigger in its normal carry position, center the grip of the gun in the web of the shooter's hand, in line with the parallel thumb and index finger, ensuring the tang (curved part) of the upper grip is in firm contact with the web.

Next, the shooter should wrap the bottom three fingers around the grip, keeping the middle finger in firm contact with the bottom of the trigger guard.

Then the shooter should extend the thumb on the opposite side of the grip to contact the tip of the middle finger, if possible. (This helps to control recoil and recovery when an individual is shooting with only one hand.) The shooter will continue by extending the index finger across the face of the trigger. For best results, the shooter's index finger should fully contact the face of the trigger to enable a full linear pull to release the firing mechanism. The individual should finish by dry-firing the pistol in a safe direction to ensure he or she can pull the trigger multiple times without restriction or adding motion to the gun.

If the shooter's index finger will not reach the trigger as previously described, the pistol in its present configuration is too large. Smaller-sized grips or a shorter-reach trigger, if available, can prove to be quite beneficial.

A few subtle changes may result in a better fit of the gun to the shooter's hand.

Conversely, if the trigger finger extends too far across the trigger to the point where it is restricted in its movement to pull the trigger, the pistol is too small for the individual's hand. If grips larger in circumference or a means of increasing trigger reach is available, the installation of either might help to optimize the hand-to-handgun fit for the shooter.

Fortunately, human hands are adaptable to a variety of gun sizes, which gives a degree of latitude in finding a gun to fit a shooter's hands.

A pistol that fits an individual correctly will ideally allow for a draw with either hand and for extension toward the target using the natural ability of eye-hand coordination. Trigger-finger placement will naturally fall to the position where pulling the trigger has no effect on the muzzle of the gun in relation to the target.

TOO BIG FOR IDEAL FIT

IDEAL FIT

TOO SMALL FOR IDEAL FIT

While being able to operate and shoot a handgun with either hand alone is recommended, it is a better idea to use both whenever possible. The strong hand, also referred to as the "dominant hand," is the one pulling the trigger. The support hand, also known as the "non-dominant hand," is the one helping the strong hand stabilize the gun on the target and performing other support duties as needed. These support duties might include changing magazines, clearing stoppages or manipulating control levers and buttons on the gun.

By maintaining a support-hand grip while shooting, a shooter maximizes surface contact with the gun to help control its movement. It is ideal for the support-hand fingers to aggressively overlap the strong-hand fingers gripping the pistol. What this infers is that the index finger of the support hand is compressed hard under the trigger guard, supporting the front of the gun. The heels of the support and strong hands are joined and compressed together to form continuous contact around the circumference of the grip. The thumb of the support hand is resting with light pressure on the side of the frame, with the thumb of the strong hand on top of and parallel with the support-hand thumb — exerting light pressure to maintain thumb-to-thumb contact during firing.

An added benefit of having the support-hand thumb resting with light pressure against the left side of the frame and the index finger in hard contact under the trigger guard is that it prevents low-left shots when a right-handed shooter does not properly manipulate the trigger (or, conversely, the opposite for a left-handed shooter when the hands are reversed).

The initial goal of an effective grip on a pistol is to maximize the surface contact between a shooter's hand(s) and the gun at all times. Grip pressure, often a controversial subject, plays a large role too. How much is enough? Can there be too much? How does someone determine the right combination? The truth is that it depends on the discipline, equipment and shooter.

How a shooter grips a gun consistently usually determines recoil control and the muzzle direction of the gun.

An analogy may be helpful here. The web and heel of a shooter's dominant hand, where the backstrap of the pistol grip is seated, is the equivalent of the stationary jaw of a shop vise. The middle joints of the fingers of either or both hands are equivalent to the movable jaw of the vise. Ideally, grip pressure should result from the fingers applying force against the frontstrap of the grip — in line with the frame and directly against the web of the hand — with minimal to no side pressure. Ideal grip pressure should be determined by the objective rather than a specific amount, which leaves too much room for personal interpretation and is rarely effective.

The gun should be held with enough force so that it doesn't shift in the shooter's hand through the firing and recovery cycles of one or more shots. The muzzle should rise and settle back to the target vertically and naturally with proper hand support. The amount of pressure generated should be consistent and sustainable for all shots fired. Too much grip pressure will restrict the range of motion of the trigger finger, making it difficult, if not impossible, to pull the trigger without moving the whole hand, which affects the muzzle's relationship to the target. Excessive grip pressure is not sustainable and wrinkles the skin, reducing the contact surface of the palm to the pistol grip and decreasing control of the pistol's movement.

In troubleshooting grip concerns, there are a few key points to remember. Controlling recoil and recovery to the target is an individual skill that is best learned through experience. The objective is to have the muzzle rise vertically, straight above the target, and settle back to the target on the same line. If the gun rises or settles on an arc or at an angle, the direction of movement has less support. This should be corrected to equalize lateral support to the gun. Some range time experimenting with grip pressure — with the muzzle lifting and settling vertically — will bring reward.

Stabilizing the Muzzle on the Target

Once a shooter has established an effective and consistent grip and body position in relation to the target, stabilizing the muzzle on the target is the next step to success.

Stabilizing the muzzle of the pistol on the target is directly related to hitting the intended location on the target within the capabilities of the gun, ammunition and shooter. Of the three, the shooter is the only real variable. The stability for which the shooter is striving is to hold the gun with minimal muzzle movement in relation to the desired impact area. Realize that a shooter is always moving to some degree, however slight. That movement is transferred to the firearm. The goal of any shooter is to minimize that movement in the time it takes to get the muzzle on target and fire the shot.

Dry-fire practice can help a shooter learn how to best stabilize a gun, regardless of discipline. The shooter can discover his or her capabilities by attaching a laser to a gun and engaging a target at expected live-fire distances. Usually, the shooter will find that reducing the tension in the body (except for the wrists and hands, which are supporting and guiding the gun) enhances muzzle stability. The shooter can practice this from a stationary position or while moving, if the circumstances dictate.

Upon being able to consistently hold the gun in the target area while minimizing movement, the shooter can add trigger pull (to replicate firing a shot) to the practice regimen. The shooter can then transition to live-fire exercises after achieving the ability to pull the trigger without adding movement to the gun. Firing groups of five or more shots will help the shooter learn what works best in stabilizing the muzzle on the target.

Since flyers usually bring to light deficiencies in a shooter's delivery system that need to be corrected, round groups with no flyers or errant shots indicate that a shooter is properly executing the biomechanical efforts of shot delivery. A shooter who is not sure why errant shots are present can unload the gun and shoot a dry group, paying maximum visual attention to the sights to reveal the problem.

Trigger Manipulation

Trigger manipulation is arguably the most important facet of pistol marksmanship. A shooter mismanipulating the trigger at the last instant of delivering a shot can move the muzzle off the target before the bullet exits the gun. The result is a bullet impacting somewhere other than where the shooter expected.

After stabilizing the muzzle on the target, the shooter must move the trigger in such a manner as to fire the gun so that it has no effect on the muzzle's position in relation to the target. For best results, the trigger's movement should be smooth and fluid. Slow or fast is of little relevance as long as the muzzle stays on the target until the bullet exits the barrel.

A new shooter or someone struggling with mastering trigger-control techniques should consider learning to control the trigger in both directions. Once the index finger contacts the trigger, it should never lose contact until that shooting cycle stops.

A single cycle of the trigger can be described as follows: Initial contact is made with the face of the trigger. The shooter's finger pressure increases to take up the slack in the trigger until it reaches the break point. Further finger pressure moves the trigger past the break point to fire the gun. Once the trigger passes the break point, it continues slightly in overtravel until pressure is released or a mechanical stop is encountered. In either case, the trigger reverses direction and is controlled forward to the point of reset. Reset is when the trigger and the internal firing mechanism reconnect, readying the gun to fire the next shot. At this point, the trigger travel is reversed once again to start the process for the next shot.

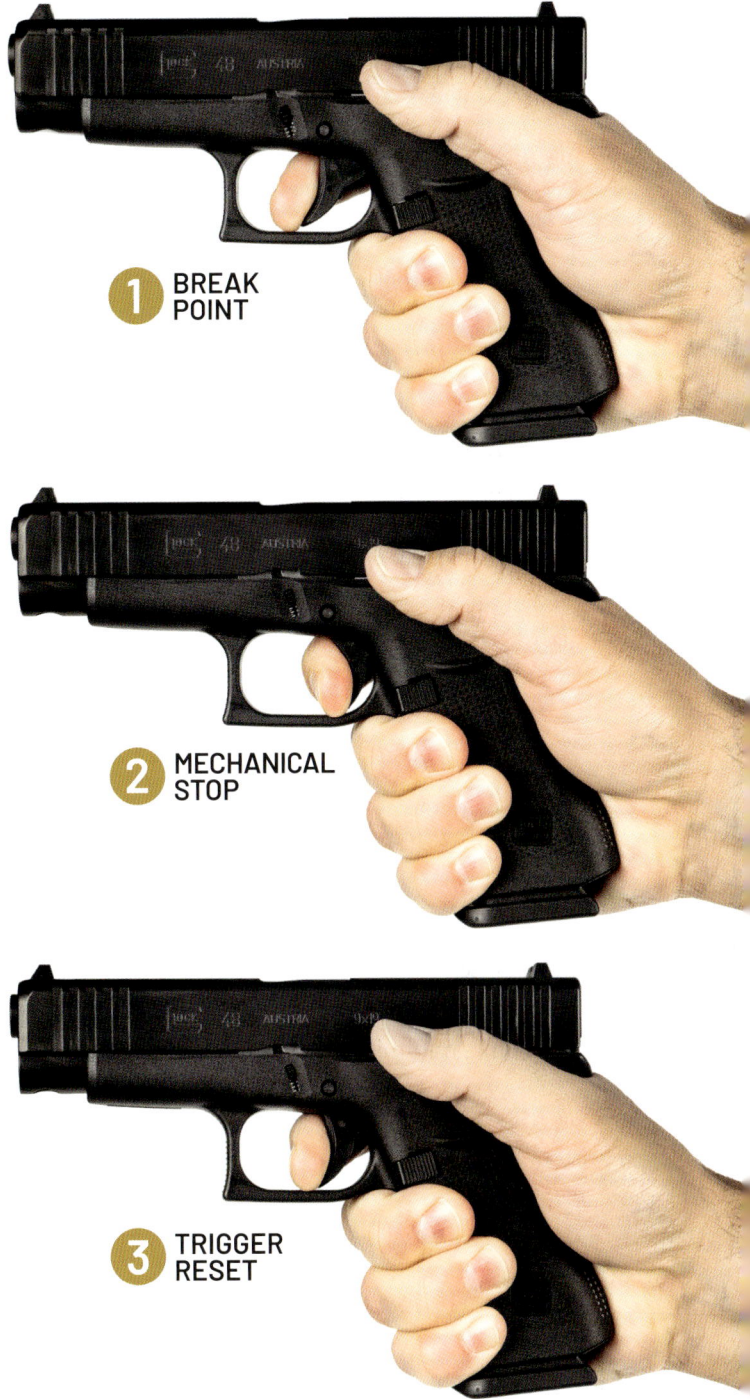

1 BREAK POINT

2 MECHANICAL STOP

3 TRIGGER RESET

For maximum efficiency in firing multiple shots, it is prudent for a shooter to coordinate trigger movement with the recoil and recovery of the gun to the target.

When the shot fires, the muzzle lifts in recoil. As the muzzle lifts, the trigger should be released forward to reset at the peak of the muzzle's upward movement.

As the muzzle settles back to the target, pressure is applied to the trigger, breaking the next shot at or near the instant the muzzle is back on the target.

Once this is perfected with conscious repetition, it becomes a very efficient means of subconsciously operating the trigger.

An alternative method sometimes preferred by a more experienced shooter is to let the trigger finger float forward of the trigger, losing contact during recoil and reset, then reengaging the trigger on recovery of the muzzle to the target.

In either case, smooth, fluid movement of the trigger is imperative to firing the gun without disturbing the relationship between the muzzle and the target.

Follow-Through

Follow-through is often discussed but is rarely understood by shooters. Follow-through is simply exercising the mental, physical and visual fundamentals of delivering a shot until the bullet exits the muzzle. Once the bullet exits the muzzle, a shooter has no influence on its impact location, and the need for follow-through has ended.

On occasion, an individual can fire a shot mentally but not mechanically. This is why it is imperative that the shooter see and recognize muzzle flash and blast as the indication that the bullet has left the barrel. This is the transition point between follow-through and recoil as the muzzle lifts off the target. The feeling of the gun pushing back in the hand as the muzzle lifts off the target is a secondary indicator that follow-through is no longer needed. Recoil ceases and recovery begins at the peak of the upward arc of the muzzle. Recovery is the time and movement necessary to get the muzzle back on the target.

Each person's biomechanical capabilities in gripping a gun, stabilizing it on the target, pulling the trigger to fire the gun, following through and recovering to the target are unique. Comprehending the objectives necessary to accomplish these tasks makes for a good starting point on which to build and improve with experience. As any good trainer will profess, there is no one way that best suits the needs of every shooter; rather, there are starting points that expand on the fundamentals and lead each shooter on a journey to success.

Improvised Shooting Positions

Improvised positions present their own set of challenges. An improvised shooting position is one that a shooter assumes in an impromptu situation, using whatever is available to his or her best advantage.

Although there are an infinite number of circumstances and positions that could have relevance, the essentials can be broken down into degrees of stability, cover or concealment, and, in some cases, movement. The following guidelines will provide a biomechanical foundation upon which any shooter can build to achieve the highest level of success when it comes to shooting from an improvised position.

An upright position is essentially a standing position that uses available objects to improve muzzle stability. It is important to remember not to rest the gun or the hands on an object — particularly if it is solid and immovable. While the object may be stable, it can also change the recoil characteristics of the gun and the impact point of the bullet on the target. Muzzle stability can be improved by leaning the torso against a stationary object or resting the arms behind the wrists against a solid support. A shooter has maximum balance and mobility while in the standing position and can easily shift in position or move to a different location.

Intermediate positions can provide a greater level of muzzle stability and adaptability to cover and concealment in limited-space environments than upright positions do. They provide flexibility in vertical-space needs while moderating mobility restrictions (depending on the technique used).

A simple technique a shooter can employ to maintain balance and muzzle stability while getting in and out of the standing position is to place both knees on the ground, keeping the torso upright and stabilizing the gun as if he or she were in the standing position. The shooter can make elevation adjustments by bending the knees and sitting on the heels for a lower profile or anywhere up to and including the upright position. The shooter can easily achieve mobility by stepping forward with one foot into the upright position again. Alternative kneeling positions, with one knee on the ground and the other knee upright, give the shooter the added benefit of being able to use the upright knee as a rest for the arms, which increases muzzle stability. The trade-off is less mobility.

The sitting position is the most stable and least mobile of the intermediate positions. The buttocks and both feet should be in contact with the ground, leaving both knees upright and in support of the arms to stabilize the pistol. This position is particularly effective in providing a shooter with a stable platform when the back is resting against a vertical surface. For someone with limited flexibility and range of motion, getting into and out of the sitting position may not be practical. Therefore, this position may not be possible for such an individual.

The most stable position without mechanical support is the prone position. It is also the least mobile and most difficult to assume. As with any of the preceding positions, it is not recommended that a shooter artificially support the gun or hands since either one can alter the bullet's impact on the target.

Using simplicity and ease of assumption as objectives, a reasonably fit individual can move from an upright position to an intermediate position and on to a prone position.

To transition from a standing position to a kneeling position, a shooter must place both knees on the ground. Everything from the knees up should remain the same. By bending at the knees, the shooter can raise and lower the gun's relationship to the target as needed.

Moving from the kneeling position to the prone position is just as simple. The shooter should keep his or her finger off the trigger and the muzzle pointed in a safe direction, leaning forward to enable the support hand to touch the ground and control the torso. Once in the prone position, the shooter should assume a two-handed grip, bringing the pistol into the line of sight. Be aware that the distance the pistol is positioned in front of the face may vary from shooter to shooter. The implications of gun movement from recoil are obvious. Sight picture may change in view but not in value if the shooter maintains sight alignment.

Recovery to the kneeling position is essentially the reverse of transitioning from kneeling to the prone position. While practicing good muzzle management and trigger-finger discipline, the shooter should use the support hand to push the upper body upright into the kneeling position. The shooter can engage the strong-side elbow for stability, paying close attention to the position and condition of the pistol to ensure safety.

A shooter has two options when transitioning from the kneeling to the standing position: either stepping off with either foot in the direction of travel or simply shifting the body weight to the toes, resuming an upright position.

Not every shooter will be able to replicate the methods as suggested. Consider, however, the adaptability of humans, what the desired result might be and how to achieve the objective in an alternate manner to be successful. Accepting that body size, range of motion, previous injuries and other obstacles sometimes prevent an individual from assuming a specific improvised position can also help to relieve a struggling shooter's frustration. Thinking in terms of upright, intermediate and prone as the objectives, a shooter can and will find a workable solution that fulfills his or her needs.

Moving and Shooting

Shooting while moving is not difficult for most people. Shooting while moving and hitting a target adds a significant challenge to the equation.

Put in the proper context, shooting while moving is most often applicable in relatively short time frames and when a shooter is in close proximity to the target. Typically, more than one shot is required, which complicates the process.

The same basic tenets of muzzle management and trigger-finger discipline apply whether the shooter is moving or not. If the objective of shooting is to hit a specific target, the muzzle must be pointed at the target when the bullet exits the muzzle.

Much has been written about how a shooter should move his or her feet, when a shooter should pull the trigger and where a shooter's eyes should be focused to ensure a hit on the target. A shooter can learn the technique in a few minutes by filling a cup or a glass up to the brim with water. While gripping the cup much like a gun held at arm's length, parallel to the floor, the individual should attempt to move in any direction without spilling any water. The stability necessary to minimize the loss of water directly correlates to how the shooter must stabilize the muzzle of a handgun on a target. The body will automatically act as a shock absorber from the feet to the elbows, allowing the hands and whatever is in them to float in space (as opposed to the erratic movement produced by rigidity in the body).

Once movement becomes fluid, with minimal water spillage, the shooter can trade the cup and water for an unloaded pistol, repeating the same movement exercises in multiple directions and noticing the outline of the pistol's slide as it floats within the outline of the target. As long as the outline of the slide is superimposed on the target, the shooter should be able to attain hits on the target in live-fire.

Before transitioning to live-fire, the shooter should also add trigger control to the movement exercises. As always for maximum effectiveness, the trigger movement should have no influence on the muzzle's position on the target. Once the dry work is satisfactory, the transition to live-fire will be surprisingly easy. When working with live ammunition, a shooter should move only as quickly as he or she can deliver accurate hits to the target. The shooter should practice in as many directions as relevant to the current or anticipated requirements. For personal defense or combat practice, an individual should incorporate shooting with the strong hand only and the support hand only. Any handling technique, such as reloading or immediate action to clear a stoppage, should also be part of a shooter's training plan and should be practiced while the shooter is moving or in an improvised position.

Ultimately, any action a student learned from a stationary position can also be learned and implemented while moving.

Economy of Motion

The phrase "economy of motion" should remain at the forefront of a shooter's efforts to perfect a shooting style or technique.

The more complicated the thought or action, the more room for error or distraction.

Biomechanically speaking, minimizing motion equates to faster performance.

When learning a new technique or action, a shooter should practice it at a speed that allows for detection and correction of any unnecessary movement from start to finish. Half speed or less is a general guideline. This allows the shooter's body to find and commit an action or movement to the subconscious mind. The action or movement then becomes automatic and highly efficient when it is initiated by an outside stimulus.

An example to further clarify this point is to examine a shooter's draw technique. A shooter will sometimes mask inefficiency in the draw by the speed in which he or she executes the action. When the shooter is able to break down the action into segments — performed in slow motion — any inefficiencies become apparent.

For instance, look at how the shooter establishes a grip while the pistol is still in the holster. A shooter might seat the web of the dominant hand firmly in the backstrap of the pistol before wrapping the fingers around the frontstrap to withdraw the pistol from the holster. This actually drives the pistol deeper into the holster, forcing it in the opposite direction of the draw before the shooter lifts it out of the holster and presents it to the target.

A shooter might consider wrapping the fingers around the frontstrap of the pistol first, using those fingers to seat the

backstrap of the grip into the web of the hand as he or she withdraws the pistol from the holster.

It's a simple change that moves the gun in one direction instead of two just to get it out of the holster.

Once the muzzle of the gun is clear of the holster, it is prudent to examine how to get the muzzle pointed at the target in the most expedient manner. Frequently, a shooter will discover that the muzzle will track in a high or low arc on the way to the target, only to actually point at the target when the drawing arm is at full extension. Following the universally accepted safety protocol of the trigger finger contacting the trigger only once the muzzle is pointed at the target (provided the shooter has made the decision to shoot at the target), efficiency of operation is lost doing one thing at a time as opposed to coordinating multiple efforts simultaneously.

A shooter should consider drawing the pistol vertically from the holster (as far as the range of motion will allow), rotating the pistol at that point so that the muzzle is on the target and driving the gun in a relatively straight line to the target (as if throwing a punch). Since the muzzle is pointing at the target from the rotation point, the shooter can touch the trigger with the trigger finger and initiate the pull while driving the gun to the target. Ideally, the sights will come into view on the target as the shooter is pulling the trigger, providing an acceptable sight picture that coincides with the shooter firing the gun at or near full extension of the arm.

This is but one example of how speed can be attained without compromising accuracy or safety.

SIMPLIFIED TO INCREASE PROFICIENCY

By becoming more aware of how and why biomechanical factors are important to shooter performance in marksmanship, an individual can more readily streamline and simplify movement and action to increase proficiency.

CHAPTER 8
DELIVERING A GOOD SHOT

A common thread among some shooters is that they do not know with certainty that the techniques they are using to hit their targets are what it takes to achieve their best performance. Are they shooting to their potential? Are there better or more efficient ways they haven't discovered? Coupled with that, shooters may not know why the techniques they're currently using work best for them. Remember that variables do apply with different types of shooting.

There are three areas of shot delivery and, when combined, specific to a discipline, they yield maximum performance for an individual. In each of these areas, a shooter needs to understand, test, validate and practice the answers to "what?," "why?" and "how?" to achieve the best results.

In any type of shooting, an individual needs to discover and understand what to see, feel and think consciously and subconsciously for each shot fired. Once the shooter understands the three areas, he or she then needs to know how to apply them efficiently and effectively.

With repetition, they become automatic actions with little to no conscious input. Ultimately, when a person recognizes a shootable target, the prior programming of the subconscious mind takes over and completes the task much faster and more accurately than were conscious thought processing the situation.

Progress is greatly enhanced if the shooter knows and understands why the techniques of application work. This includes dry-firing and live-firing, practicing mental techniques, and analogizing with other similar activities.

The knowledge, understanding and successful application of a method or technique brings confidence in performance, minimizes distraction, provides a pathway to follow for success, and makes self-diagnosis for flaws or deviations in shot delivery definable and correctable.

Though each individual shooter will find minor differences in how to achieve the desired performance, a base understanding of what, how and why is relatively constant.

SEE

What a shooter sees in recognizing a target provides input to the brain, which immediately searches the mental catalog of previous experiences for the most relevant and efficient means of negotiating that target or one like it. This catalog of previous experiences can come from practical programming through physical practice, live experience or detailed visualization pertaining to the subject matter. This can also include vicarious observation, such as through videos or other media. Either the shooter finds a plausible solution to properly engage the target in the appropriate manner or draws a blank due to lack of relevant information. When drawing a blank, the shooter needs to employ conscious thought in an attempt to analyze, assess and address the challenge. This can take valuable time — perhaps more time than is available. Eventually, if time permits, a shooter should select a solution to the problem, which leads to the decision of what happens next. This decision in the brain sends signals out to the various parts of the body to act, marshaling a response to the target. The less complicated the action to solve the problem, the higher the likelihood of success.

Defining "must-haves" versus "would-like-to-haves" in training the brain for shooting engagements simplifies placing shots on the target.

For instance, the eye recognizes a legitimate target, which alerts the brain to stimulate the appropriate body parts to stabilize the muzzle of the gun on the target and pull the trigger to hit it.

Speed is always a consideration when there are time constraints — but especially when precision is factored in too. Speed is simply the economy of thought and motion when an individual is performing a task, such as hitting a target. Applying only what is necessary and avoiding what is not will generate success in the most efficient and expedient manner.

A good principle to follow pertaining to this train of thought is that the first sight picture is almost always the best sight picture. Trying to fine-tune the first sight picture interrupts the flow of executing the shot and degrades maximizing the potential of the hit. This leads to other distractions and problems that arise when a shooter is engaging multiple targets, targets with multiple shots, or multiple shots on multiple targets.

The basic tenet for a shooter to remember when firing multiple shots, whether that's two or 20, is to shoot only as fast as he or she can produce hits.

When misses take place, the shooter's eyes, mind and body are out of synchronization. For instance, if the brain signals the body to pull the trigger without input from the eyes as to where the sights are when the trigger is pulled, misses will likely happen, which stimulates the body to shoot faster to make up for the missed shots. This usually results in more missed shots, compounding the lack of success and creating a vicious cycle of failure.

Another example is the eye registering an acceptable sight picture and sending it to the brain, which in turn sends an urgent impulse to the hand and index finger that the sights are right and that the shot must go before they are not on the target anymore. Therefore, the hand convulses, the trigger finger jerks the trigger — trying to keep up — and the muzzle moves off the target before the bullet exits the barrel. More-intense focus on the sights and a little patience in pulling the trigger by practicing strict mental discipline will fix the problem.

It should be apparent that the brain, body and eyes need to work in concert to achieve the best shooting results.

Given that the two essentials to hitting a target are to get the sights, and therefore the muzzle, on the target and to pull the trigger with little to no effect on the position of the sights to each other or the target, the brain has two things to synchronize with similar levels of attention.

Training to do this is simple but does require consistent mental attention to attain repeatability from shot to shot.

Ultimately, the shooter's eye identifies the target, signaling the brain to move the hands to position the sights on the target, thus forming the sight picture. As this is taking place, the trigger finger contacts the trigger and applies pressure as the sights settle on the target. To keep the brain from devoting too much attention to either the sights or the trigger, the shooter's mental attention and visual attention must be equally divided by imagining a mechanical connection between the trigger and the front sight. With iron sights, the trigger pulls the front sight toward the eye — as if it were on a rail — while keeping it properly positioned in the rear-sight notch. With a red-dot sight, the connection is between the trigger and the red dot,

pulling the dot to the center of the eye. In either case, a shooter's mental focus is applied equally to the two essentials of hitting the target, maximizing effort and minimizing distraction.

It is critical to keep in mind that the eye initiates the shot by stimulating the brain to bring the body into action. The continual input of an acceptable sight picture of the target to be engaged, the muzzle flash and brass ejection as each shot is discharged to ensure sufficient follow-through, and the muzzle lifting in recoil and settling on the next target should all be familiar to an accomplished shooter. Understanding and utilizing central and peripheral vision (as the conditions dictate) to make successful hits greatly enhances a shooter's versatility in all aspects of using a handgun. Using the natural ability of eye-hand coordination is one of the best-kept shooting secrets. It is an undeniable fact that it can be cultivated to broaden and improve a shooter's skill in hitting a target within most any time frame.

FEEL

In addressing what a shooter needs to feel while shooting a handgun, the subjects of spatial awareness and sense of touch are important.

Spatial awareness refers to the body position a shooter assumes while pointing a handgun at a target. Ideally, it is as natural as pointing a finger at an object. However, with the variety of grip sizes and angles available, some adjustments may have to be made to fit the characteristics of the shooter's anatomy to get the muzzle pointed at the target. For instance,

when a shooter adds a red-dot sight to a pistol, it is very common for that pistol to point high, making the dot hard to find initially. A shooter can remedy this problem by adjusting the arms and hands to get the dot on the target and by developing and remembering this position. A sense of balance for the maximum mitigation of body movement and, in other cases, to be able to move fluidly in any direction with equal ease are additional examples of spatial awareness.

Like with other types of physical conditioning, repetition and attention to detail commit the needed information to the brain's memory bank for future use.

Another aspect to the "feel" segment of the equation relates to the sense of touch — specifically the hands. The hands are incredibly sensitive in applying varying degrees of pressure, determining dimension and executing movement as separate or collective components.

During shooting, one or both hands hold the gun on the target, pull the trigger without affecting the hold, control recoil at discharge, and repeat as needed. It sounds simple, but there are as many variables involved as there are hands and fingers that need to be considered for maximum performance.

Gripping the gun consistently from shot to shot is imperative for accurate shooting. But defining proper grip on a handgun can be challenging. Even seasoned instructors have their favorite descriptions, but grip is not a one-size-fits-all application. Understanding the objective of a specific application or how a shooter's hands typically operate and function can be beneficial.

One could easily compare gripping a handgun to gripping a golf club, hammer or baseball bat. The objective with each is to maintain a high level of control in relation to a separate object, either moving or stationary. Held too loosely, the tool will slip in the hand. Held too tightly, the smooth, fluid movement necessary to maximize performance in impacting the second object will be restricted due to excess muscle tension.

For example, start three nails in a piece of lumber several inches apart. While holding the hammer as loosely as possible without it slipping out of the hand, drive the first nail until it is fully seated, counting the number of impacts necessary to accomplish the task. Then repeat the exercise while holding the hammer with as much muscle tension as possible when impacting the nail. Note the number of impacts required to seat the nail. Also record the misses. Finally, repeat the exercise again, holding the hammer with a comfortable, firm grip that is sustainable over several minutes. The best success typically comes from the last repetition.

Describing a firm grip is somewhat elusive, but try to envision shaking hands with someone after coming to an agreement.

The correct grip is one that controls the pistol as it rises and settles vertically from sight picture to sight picture without it slipping in the hands or needing to be adjusted between shots. This should continue for as long as the series of shots is fired.

Maximum contact between the hands and the gripping surfaces of the gun and the pressure exerted on those surfaces maximize control and minimize the need for adjusting hand position during shooting.

For optimal performance, a shooter's pressure on the grip must be consistent from the first shot to the last.

A common error regarding grip involves a shooter varying the pressure of individual fingers while pulling the trigger. Since the hand and fingers are designed to

work together when gripping an object, it is difficult, in the absence of training, to move the index finger and fire a shot without changes in grip pressure from the rest of the fingers. Dry-fire training — in particular, the "Wall Drill," where the sights and trigger are given maximum attention — will help a shooter isolate and eliminate changing grip during the trigger stroke.

Trigger manipulation or operation is another of those active components of shooting that has a mind-boggling number of descriptions in the firearms community. There are two different methods of moving the trigger to create discharge, both of which accomplish essentially the same thing using different techniques.

In either case, the trigger finger should have, at a minimum, full contact across the face of the trigger in order to move the trigger rearward, firing the gun, without inducing lateral pressure. The speed in which the trigger moves can be fast or slow — as long as the muzzle's position relative to the target is not affected. Once the trigger releases the firing mechanism, the shooter has two paths from which to choose to ready the gun for the next shot.

The first choice is to control the trigger forward until it resets and reconnects with the firing mechanism, preparing the trigger for the next shot. Using this method, the trigger finger never loses contact with the trigger — from start to finish — until the series of shots is complete. This method is recommended for a foundational shooter on up as a means of keeping trigger movement independent from the rest of the hand.

The second choice is to operate the trigger quickly rearward to cause a discharge and then allow

1 TRIGGER RESET CONTROLLED BY FINGER CONTACT

2 INDEPENDENT RESET WITHOUT FINGER CONTACT

the trigger to reset independently without finger contact. An experienced shooter capable of extreme speed and accuracy can use this technique successfully without affecting the muzzle's relationship to the target.

The key with either method is to isolate trigger-finger movement, pressure and distance of travel from the rest of the hand to preserve the desired sight picture as the shooter operates the trigger.

When it's used effectively, the support or non-dominant hand can greatly enhance a shooter's marksmanship ability. A good starting point is to establish the shooting grip with the dominant hand and overlay the non-dominant hand with the index finger tight under the trigger guard. This positions the fingers of both hands parallel to one another for maximum strength. The thumbs of both hands are stacked and pointed forward. They may touch the side of the frame for lateral support, if desired, but should not contact the semi-auto's slide or revolver's cylinder.

Grip pressure with the support hand should be greater than that of the dominant hand to maximize muzzle stability and to free up the trigger finger for optimal trigger control.

The feel of the support hand's position and pressure should become second nature any time a shooter holds the gun on a target with two hands. Just as when drawing from the holster or simply picking up a familiar gun, the feel of the gun puts it in the proper position for best performance. This comes from repetition and knowing what, how and why it works.

THINK

The thought process in delivering a good shot does not need to be complicated. In fact, the less conscious the thought and the more subconscious the programming, the better for the shooter.

How a shooter arrives at what it takes to deliver a good shot comes from doing the work in defining what he or she wanted to accomplish, how it was done and why the plan worked.

After the mechanics are practiced and proven, the thought process manages the coordination of vision and biomechanical effort with a hint of other senses to add substance to the response to a stimulus.

Visualization of the mechanics in as much detail as necessary for the mental duplication of a shot or series of shots is helpful in programming the subconscious to respond immediately and accurately to a stimulus or cue.

One of the keys to information being downloaded and accepted from the cognitive mind into the subconscious mind for instant retrieval is that it is simple, understandable and indisputable for the application. That way, there is no hesitation or question to delay the action or perhaps cause failure.

A case in point stems from the premise that muzzle management and trigger control are all that are really necessary to hit a target. If the muzzle is pointed at a target at any reasonable handgun distance when the bullet exits, there is no argument that the bullet will hit the target — aside from an act of God. So, in essence, if the shooter can point the gun at a target and operate the trigger to fire the gun without affecting the muzzle's relationship to the target, that is all that is necessary to hit the target. It is indisputable. Certainly, there are many things that can be added to improve consistency or hit placement on the target, but the muzzle still has to be pointed at the target to do that.

One of the most challenging things for a shooter to do is to maintain mental discipline during the shooting process. What this means is keeping the conscious mind under control while letting the subconscious mind do what it has been trained to do. It is almost like giving the conscious mind something to do to keep it out of trouble while permitting the subconscious to work.

Often, a successful shooter will have key words or phrases he or she repeats to initiate shot delivery and continue through the last shot to prevent errant thoughts from entering the mind and corrupting the shot sequence. Visual and sometimes audible cues are used to avoid distraction. These phrases or cues are effective when an unanticipated distraction raises its ugly head and the shooter needs to refocus to accomplish a task.

A good technique worth repeating to keep distractions to a minimum when shooting a pistol or revolver is as follows:
- Place the sights in the middle of the target.
- Imagine a mechanical connection between the trigger and the front sight.
- Focus hard visually on the center of the front sight through the window of the rear-sight notch.
- Place the trigger finger on the trigger.
- Envision pulling the front sight through the rear-sight notch with the trigger while keeping that front sight aligned within the notch until the gun fires.

The beauty of this technique is that it combines visual, physical and mental attention to work on the two most critical parts of shot delivery simultaneously.

Another recommended technique to assist in perfecting visual attention for precision shooting and ensuring follow-through is the "Smoke, Flash and Brass Drill." Each time the gun fires, smoke and muzzle flash take place the instant the bullet leaves the muzzle. Since the front sight is a minimal distance above the muzzle, the shooter should easily see the smoke and flash around the front sight if his or her eyes are open and focused on the front of the gun.

In between the front sight and the rear sight is the ejection port, from which spent brass is ejected every time the gun fires. If the shooter's eyes are open and truly focused on the front sight through the rear-sight notch, he or she will easily notice the ejected brass as it exits the ejection port as the slide cycles. In the case of a revolver, the flash at the barrel-cylinder gap serves the same purpose.

For a shooter who has the mechanics of shooting sufficiently mastered and the mental programming progressing at a satisfactory level, there are other steps that can lead to improved shooting performance. For the target shooter or hunter, thinking about where the bullet needs to hit will put it there if nothing else is present to influence the flight of the bullet. For the seasoned precision shooter, "thinking center" is an age-old trick to edge out the mechanically sound but less experienced competitors.

The mental game of shooting is limited only by a shooter's imagination. Much has yet to be discovered about the mental aspects of shooting. Therefore, if it works, there is nothing wrong with applying it.

CONTINUING EDUCATION

Every shooter, regardless of discipline, is unique and has different skills and life experiences from which to draw. By factoring in what he or she needs to see, feel and think as it relates to a perpetual awareness of the changes that result in improved performance, a shooter never stops learning and evolving in a chosen endeavor. Whether a beginner or a seasoned pro on the firing line, a shooter should always be a student.

CHAPTER 9
THE DIFFERENT DISCIPLINES

Overall, shooting a pistol and hitting the intended target is a pretty simple process. All that needs to happen is for the shooter to stabilize the muzzle on the target and cause the gun to fire without affecting the muzzle's stability.

However, when circumstances such as time, distance, target size, multiple shots, multiple targets or adversaries, atmospheric conditions, and shooting positions are factored in — not to mention the potential rules of the encounter — achieving the best level of performance becomes more complicated.

These factors create variables in shooting that are categorized and classified as specific shooting objectives. There is a degree of overlap from one discipline to another, but there are also notable differences that determine how to achieve success for the task at hand.

PRECISION MARKSMANSHIP

Precision marksmanship is the measured performance required to extract a consistent, repetitive result out of a shooter and the shooter's equipment and ammunition under a set standard. The goal of precision marksmanship is to put all of the shots fired in the desired location on a target and into the smallest group possible with the equipment being used.

An example is the "Bullet Hole Drill" discussed in detail in Chapter 12. The shooter's goal is to fire the first hole in what he or she perceives as the center of the target and then place subsequent shots into the same location — that perceived center — so that there is a single bullet-diameter hole in the target.

An alternative would be to use the initial hole in the target (as opposed to the center of the target) as the point of aim. The difference is that the resulting group may impact in a different location on the target but should still be a single hole separate from the original one.

It pays to shoot both methods, as each has its merits. Each will help improve a shooter's visual and mental performance when precision is the objective. This exercise collectively tests the shooter, gun and ammunition for consistent, repetitive performance in achieving a desired result.

A shooter should test the handgun and ammunition beforehand from a bench or in a machine rest farther away — usually 25 or 50 yards — to validate their intrinsic capabilities. This will help the shooter differentiate between human error and equipment. It is important that the equipment perform at least as well and preferably better than the shooter using

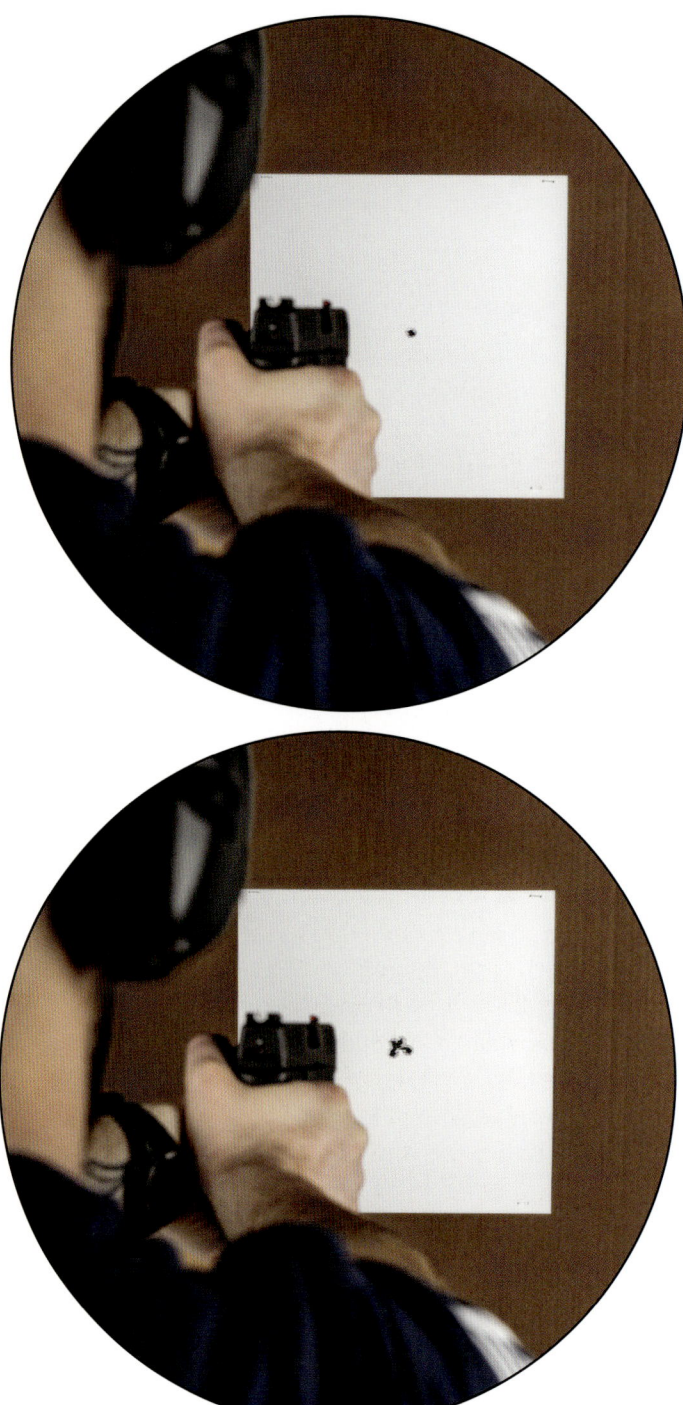

it. This leaves the shooter as the only part of the equation in precision shooting that can improve and develop consistency in achieving the desired results.

While precision may be one of the major principles of shooting, when time becomes a factor, compromises are often made. Typically, when the time allotted to shoot a target decreases, the level of precision also diminishes.

In competitive shooting, for example, the size of the target's scoring areas and the distance from which the target must be engaged drives the speed with which the shooter can successfully engage the target with the necessary precision.

NRA Precision Pistol competition is a classic example of how precision and speed are combined with distance to test a competitor's shooting ability.

The precision portion of the match, typically referred to as "Slow Fire," requires a shooter to fire at 50 yards at a target with a 3 3/8-inch 10-ring (and an even smaller 1 5/8-inch X-ring for breaking ties). The shooting position is standing, using one hand only. The shooter is allowed a total of 10 minutes to fire 10 shots.

There are two speed portions of the NRA Precision Pistol competition. They use the same size scoring rings on the target as Slow Fire but at half the distance. The first speed-oriented course of fire is referred to as "Timed Fire." Timed Fire is fired in two five-shot strings in which the shooter has 20 seconds to shoot each string.

Timed Fire is followed by what's called "Rapid Fire." This course of fire uses the same type of target as in the Timed Fire course. It too is fired in five-shot strings, but a shooter is given only 10 seconds for each string.

Pistols used in this type of competition fall within their individual categories, including .22 Rimfire, Centerfire (.32 caliber and above), .45 ACP and Service Pistol. In recent years, the Service Pistol category, as defined by the Civilian Marksmanship Program, has expanded the number of pistols qualifying for that category to almost any 9mm or larger caliber semi-automatic pistol with a trigger weighing at least 4 pounds and a barrel length not exceeding 5.4 inches. This allows individuals with law enforcement, security and concealed carry service pistols to compete in the Excellence in Competition (EIC) matches (in which points are earned by the top-scoring competitors toward the coveted Distinguished Pistol Shot Badge) without having to purchase match-specific equipment.

Each course of fire has its own challenges that require a shooter to blend precision with speed to optimize overall performance while shooting a complete match with the handgun of his or her choice.

COMBAT AND DEFENSIVE MARKSMANSHIP

There are two organizations popular in today's competitive shooting disciplines that use pistols and revolvers designed primarily for defensive and combat purposes. They have enough differences to be governed under different sets of rules, but both use a composite of accuracy, speed and measured power to achieve their goals. This adds the dimension of power, which is rarely a factor in Precision Pistol competition.

Photo courtesy of CMP Archives

These two organizations are the International Defensive Pistol Association (IDPA) and the United States Practical Shooting Association (USPSA).

The IDPA is more oriented to the shooter who prefers to hone his or her skills with equipment typically used when carrying concealed. In fact, the majority of its shooting exercises begin from concealment.

Handguns chambered in 9mm Parabellum or .38 Special are considered the starting point for defensive usage in many circles, including the IDPA. There are various IDPA classes to accommodate the many choices a person has in the selection of a concealed carry handgun, as long as it is 9mm Parabellum or larger in caliber or power.

There are two categories that challenge the competitor's marksmanship and practical skills: the "Standard" and "Scenario" stages.

The Standard stages are designed to test a shooter's performance of various techniques employed in IDPA shooting. Target distances range from a safe distance of a few feet to 50 yards, depending on the size and composition of the target.

The Scenario stages are designed to replicate actual real-world scenarios relevant to a street encounter that a competitor might actually experience. Target distances range from a safe distance of several feet to 20 yards, with 75 percent of the shots falling within 15 yards of the shooter. The variables are conceivably infinite as long as the scenarios are safe to shoot and fall within the organizational guidelines.

Photo courtesy of IDPA and Jeff Melchior

The standard cardboard target for IDPA competition has a scoring area of roughly 30 by 17 3/8 inches. In order to maximize marksmanship performance, a shooter must ensure that all shots contact either an 8-inch-diameter down-zero ring in the body of the target or a 4-inch down-zero ring in the head of the target.

While marksmanship is an important part of shooting in general, the speed with which it is delivered is considered in scoring an IDPA target in competition. Formulas for scoring in IDPA competition include the value of hits on the target as well as the time it takes to make those hits. Both are factored in to determine a competitor's total score.

IDPA competition is a great way to practice combining marksmanship skills with other shooting skills, such as movement, firing from improvised positions and hitting multiple targets under time. The shooter will realize and come to appreciate the comprehensive balance of skills that are necessary to achieve success.

Similar to the IDPA is the USPSA. The USPSA is the American offshoot of the International Practical Shooting Confederation (IPSC), which is recognized as the sanctioning body worldwide for practical shooting.

USPSA shooters have a wider range of equipment options when it comes to firearms, holsters, magazines and accessories than do IDPA shooters. The rules, range setups, targets and scoring methods are dissimilar as well. Shooting from concealment is not a requirement nor a recommendation when shooting USPSA matches.

Photo courtesy of USPSA and Shannon Smith

The two organizations' root objectives focus on accuracy — combined with speed of application with a handgun — to neutralize an adversary in combat conditions.

The benefit to a shooter practicing either or both of these disciplines is learning to smoothly flow from pure accuracy to pure speed and anywhere in between on demand. Keeping in mind that a prudent shooter shoots only as fast as he or she can deliver hits to a target, the visual input of target size and distance, combined with an acceptable sight picture, tells the trigger finger how fast to pull the trigger without overdriving the gun and missing shots.

Both IDPA and USPSA competitions are good vehicles from which to learn and practice techniques that require the blend of speed and accuracy. An additional benefit is that they vary on a sliding scale as the match conditions unfold — similar to what someone might experience in a gunfight on the street.

The next level of marksmanship training — particularly for an individual who carries a gun every day for professional or personal reasons — is reality-based training. Reality-based training puts every skill learned in handling and shooting a handgun to the test by trial under fire. This type of training goes by several titles, but regardless of what it is called, the objective is to enter into a relevant and realistic scenario against an opponent.

This is done with the highest level of safety, practiced by way of equipment and scenario control, to ensure a quality experience with minimal to no injury as a result. The types of firearms and ammunition used in this training vary somewhat, but that's by design. Rounds will leave a mark, verifying hits and causing a degree of pain. Therefore, a shooter will likely want to avoid being shot at all costs.

An added dimension of this training is the dynamic nature of having to think in real time in an ever-changing set of conditions. The goal is to operate under the pressure of dealing with living, thinking opponents and to perform previously learned skills in an acceptable manner, yielding a positive outcome.

The scenarios are infinite and challenging. They help to detect and correct a participant's shortcomings and operational deficiencies that may not have been recognized previously in training or on the street.

The one thing that every shooter needs to remember is the objective of shooting. That objective is to hit the intended target as much and as often as necessary to accomplish one's goal.

In a lethal-force encounter, shot placement is crucial to stop the hostile action of an adversary at the earliest possible moment. Skill with a pistol (marksmanship) is essential to achieving success in this situation.

It is paramount to know where to shoot and to be able to assess and engage the best available target without hesitation.

While precision shot placement on a target is desirable, it may not be possible in a combat or defensive encounter, where the conditions are perpetually changing.

Hits to the central nervous system — particularly to the brain and the upper spinal cord — are most desirable. These usually result in the instant cessation of hostile activity; however, those areas are difficult to hit in a dynamic environment.

Without a neurological hit, the next best thing is to reduce the flow of oxygenated blood to the brain, which negatively affects body function. This can be accomplished by interrupting blood flow or decreasing the lungs' ability to oxygenate the blood (or both). Multiple hits in different locations on the target tend to increase the speed with which the shots can be delivered and increase the damage to the target. This increases the likelihood of quickly stopping the aggressor, which is the objective.

Taking the time to attempt to put all shots in a tiny group is counterproductive. It wastes time that may not be available and may decrease the amount of disrupted tissue created due to all of the shots going into a single opening.

In the case of combat-skill development, it is the combination of marksmanship, accuracy, sufficient power and the speed with which shots can be delivered that most often yields the best results.

RECREATIONAL MARKSMANSHIP

Recreational shooting is an ever-increasing avocation in today's society that is growing at an unprecedented rate. Recreational shooters range from first-time gun buyers who purchase handguns today because they fear they may not have the opportunity later to serious hunters who use handguns to put meat on the table to feed their families.

The foundational skills are similar for each type of gun owner. The individual starts with nomenclature and handling the gun even before ammunition is introduced into the equation. This initiates safe handling and communication about the gun, its parts and how it operates.

Once safe handling is part of a gun owner's awareness, the introduction to marksmanship comes next. It can be simple or complicated, depending on who is making the introduction. From my perspective, the simpler the better. However, the objective remains the same: hitting the target. Optimally, the foundational elements of marksmanship should be taught dry prior to the introduction of ammunition into the equation. Once a shooter becomes accustomed to the sound of the gun and the feel of the gun when it fires, the ability to hit the target on demand takes precedence.

Marksmanship goals and objectives become a matter of what a shooter classifies as "success." For the casual plinker, just being able to hit informal targets, such as soda cans 10 feet away, may accomplish the goal. For a beginner considering using a handgun for personal protection, hitting a man-sized target at 7 yards may satisfy the objective until the shooter wants to improve his or her skills with further training. This may involve working from holsters (concealed or otherwise), shooting and moving, shooting from improvised positions, and on through reality-based training scenarios, but marksmanship takes the lead throughout because the objective of shooting always remains hitting the target.

For the hunter, marksmanship may be viewed as more than just being able to hit the target. Ethically, the shooter has a responsibility to take the animal, cleanly, with a single shot to a lethal location. A shooter who has any doubt about making the shot shouldn't take it unless it is a life-or-death situation.

Gauging one's practical ability to make the shot on a game animal is relatively simple. If the heart or lung area of the game animal is the target, being able to hit the size or diameter of that area consistently with a gun suitable in caliber and power determines the maximum range for the shooter to attempt to ethically take the animal.

As an example, a white-tailed deer has a heart/lung diameter of approximately 8 inches. The maximum distance that a hunter should attempt harvesting a deer equates to the distance from which he or she can hit an 8-inch target consistently with a powerful handgun capable of delivering a lethal shot to a deer-sized animal. This distance will vary with the position the hunter uses to stabilize the gun as well as the environmental and mental pressure of taking a game animal with a handgun. Without good marksmanship skills, successful hunting is hard to imagine, much less accomplish.

The answer is to stabilize the muzzle on the target and keep it as still as possible under the given conditions and to release the shot by moving the trigger without affecting the muzzle's stability on the target.

This statement is indisputable. When the objective is precision shooting, the speed with which the shooter operates the trigger is irrelevant as long as the stability of the muzzle on the target isn't affected. There comes a point when speed starts to affect the muzzle's stability in relation to the target, which then requires the shooter to prioritize and decide which is more important: precise accuracy or speed.

Marksmanship, defined within a specific discipline, is essential to successful shooting when the objective is to hit the target.

WHAT'S ABSOLUTELY NECESSARY

Regardless of the application or the discipline of using a pistol, marksmanship is what determines a shooter's success or failure. Although there are many tricks, techniques, gadgets and other influences available to enhance one's ability to hit a target, a shooter must define what is absolutely necessary to fulfill the objective, excluding all other considerations.

CHAPTER 10
THE IMPORTANCE OF GOOD EQUIPMENT

Every shooter has to start somewhere to become a good marksman. The gun and equipment with which an individual begins may not be ideal to serve the intended purpose. More often than not, a shooter's startup equipment is what he or she had access to, got a good deal on or thinks looks cool, or it came as a suggestion from another. In many cases, a shooter without a specific goal or discipline in mind chooses a general-purpose gun and accompanying equipment based on the preceding criteria. This makes equipment selection fairly broad when it comes to finding something satisfactory with which to start. Commonly, a beginning shooter is most concerned with finding a gun, some ammunition and a few accessories.

There are multiple stages and evolutions in the progression of becoming a better shooter that will narrow the field of equipment selection as an individual gains experience. To be sure, this depends on the purpose and discipline to which the shooter decides to dedicate both time and effort. A definition of good equipment at any stage in a shooter's progression is equipment that supports and improves overall performance rather than hinders it.

There are some items that are important for every shooter, regardless of discipline, with which an individual should get started, such as safety and range gear. These, along with guns and ammo, are essential to any shooting endeavor.

SAFETY GEAR

When it comes to equipment selection, the first thing a shooter must consider is safety. The question to ask should be: Is it serviceable for its intended purpose?

Eye protection is a must. Considering that humans are issued only two eyes at birth — without the opportunity for replacements if catastrophic damage were to occur — eye protection should be a top priority.

Any eye protection is better than no eye protection. However, when it comes to shooting, safety glasses certified ANSI Z87 or better are essential to maintaining visual integrity. The American National Standards Institute, or ANSI, tests and rates safety glasses for impact resistance, penetration resistance and other capabilities related to their use. Sunglasses and everyday prescription glasses, unless they are Z87 or higher, are not sufficient to protect a shooter's eyes during shooting.

Safety glasses for shooting should have the lenses contoured to give protection above, below and to the sides of the eyes, preventing flying objects from directly and indirectly entering the eyes.

Safety glasses are available with a shooter's prescription ground directly into the lenses or with auxiliary inserts mounted on the undersides of the safety lenses. Safety glasses are offered with lenses in a multitude of colors to enhance a shooter's visibility of the sights and the target. These lenses will maximize the visual performance of the shooter in a wide variety of bright, dark and contrasting range conditions. In the beginning, plain, clear eye protection with the appropriate safety rating will serve the shooter well until experience and direction necessitate an upgrade to something more beneficial for a specific need.

Ear protection is high on the list of safety equipment too. Once the sense of hearing is permanently damaged — from shooting or any other loud noises — there is no getting it back. With the many products and devices available to protect shooters' hearing today, there is little reason for hearing loss due to gun noise.

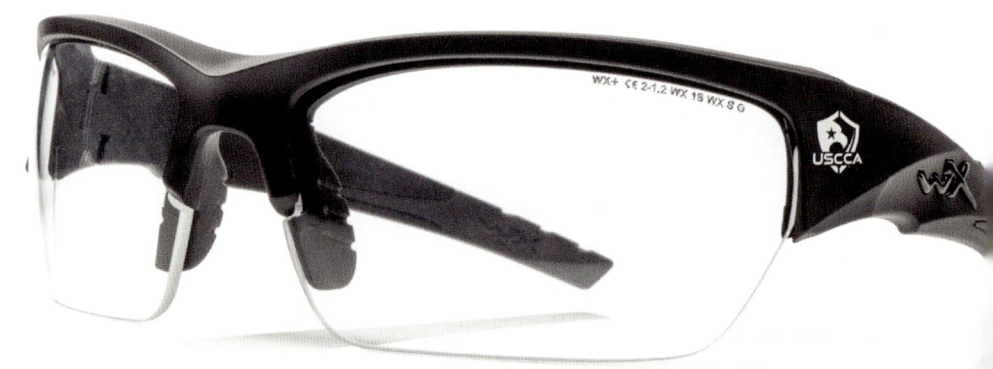

There are two popular types of hearing protection available for shooters: earplugs and earmuffs.

Earplugs, which are inserted into the opening of each ear, are economical and effective — provided they seal the ear canal once they've been inserted.

Earmuffs provide noise protection by covering the ears fully to reduce the level of sound entering them. In order for the muffs to be effective, they need to seal the area around the outside of each ear to attenuate the sound.

Both earplugs and earmuffs are available as passive hearing protection or as electronic noise-cancelling hearing protection.

Passive hearing protection decreases all noise within a shooter's hearing range. Electronic, noise-cancelling ear protection allows a shooter to hear conversation-level noise but blocks noise at levels that would damage his or her hearing.

The amount of sound reduction for both earmuffs and earplugs is measured on the Noise Reduction Rating (NRR) scale. Desirable levels of noise reduction range from the high 20s to the low 30s. For the best hearing protection, earmuffs and earplugs can be used in tandem or in a combination of passive and electronic. A shooter should never skimp on hearing protection. It takes only one incident to incur permanent hearing loss.

Aside from procuring the best eye and ear protection, a shooter can follow some general guidelines for range wear that will make the overall shooting experience safe, educational and enjoyable.

A brimmed hat or cap with the brim forward to protect the face from the sun, rain and flying objects (such as ejected brass) provides an extra layer of protection for a shooter. A closed-neck long-sleeved shirt provides protection much like a hat does. With the addition of a scarf or small hand towel around the neck, a shooter can maximize protection of the upper body from brass burns, the sun and flying objects.

Long pants, with belt loops to accommodate, at a minimum, a sturdy 1 1/2-inch belt, and pockets that make it easy to insert and retrieve things, are beneficial range wear. They should be loose-fitting, preferably with some elasticity, to accommodate ease of movement and assuming, as well as exiting, improvised positions.

The belt should be able to support the weight of a gun and holster, magazine pouches with loaded magazines, a flashlight, and other accessories as deemed necessary without collapsing or losing its shape. The length of the belt should be several inches longer than a dress belt to accommodate the holster and attachments comfortably. A belt that is infinitely adjustable will maximize and enhance the belt's fit and function as opposed to a belt with fixed adjustments.

Shoes should fully cover the feet and have soles compatible with negotiating the uneven terrain of a shooting range. Socks should not only protect the feet but also provide maximum comfort when the shooter is standing for long periods of time.

All of the clothing recommendations can be adjusted as needed to accommodate the weather conditions, but a shooter should always keep safety in perspective. With experience, a shooter will be able to select clothing for function, comfort and safety with confidence.

GUNS AND AMMO

When it comes to a firearm and the ammunition and ancillary gear that go with it at the foundational level, it is easy to define what makes up good equipment.

First and foremost, the gun must be safe and serviceable. A function check and an accuracy test will usually determine if it is.

It also helps for the shooter to have a goal or plan as to what his or her current objective is. Be mindful that the shooter's initial goals and objectives will probably change, making flexibility and open-mindedness beneficial.

Deciding on a gun with which to start involves availability, familiarity and an intended application.

If this is a shooter's first handgun, a foundational class for familiarization with the types and usages of pistols and revolvers would be the first place to start. Just being able to know the differences between a revolver's and a semi-automatic's operation and how each is handled and maintained will enlighten and guide the first-time handgun owner.

Ideally, being able to shoot pistols and revolvers prior to purchasing one will go far in the decision-making process. A gun shop that has a range and a "try before you buy" program gives a new shooter an opportunity to handle and fire prospective firearms before making a final decision. It is important to remember that this initial purchase may not — and probably won't — be a one-and-done addition. As time passes and a shooter gains experience, interests and objectives may also change. That might require a different type of firearm than the shooter originally purchased.

When buying a handgun and associated accessories for the first or 10th time, a shooter should consider a few basic guidelines that can be helpful in leading the individual to make the best decision.

Application should be the chief consideration. Why does the shooter want the gun or gear? What is its purpose? How will it help the shooter achieve these goals? Is this the best option for the price? These types of questions will help the shooter to maintain focus and acquire acceptable, if not the best, equipment for the intended application or area of interest.

To recap the basic premise of marksmanship, the objective of shooting is to hit the target. The size and fit of a gun to a shooter's hands becomes a primary concern. Fitting the gun to the hands contributes to a shooter's ability to hit a target by capitalizing on the natural attribute of eye-hand coordination. Eye-hand coordination allows a shooter to point at anything he or she sees, which puts the gun on the target prior to the individual fine-tuning its position by aligning the sights.

Fitting a gun is little more than placing the grip of the pistol or revolver in the web of the hand, between the thumb and index finger, so that the barrel points where the index finger points. An equally important consideration is where the index finger (the trigger finger) sits in relation to the trigger. Aside from getting the gun pointed at the target, a shooter must be able to pull the trigger to fire the gun without affecting the position of the gun on the target. This can usually be accomplished if the trigger finger extends across the face of the trigger sufficiently, allowing the shooter to pull it in line with the frame to release the shot.

When using this method to fit a gun, a shooter can discover the optimal size of the grip and the reach of the trigger finger to achieve the best performance in almost any discipline.

The weight of the gun with a full complement of ammunition can have an impact on gun selection. If the gun is too heavy for a shooter to maintain stability on the target when the arms are fully extended in a typical shooting position, success won't be forthcoming without some strength-building exercises.

At the opposite end of the spectrum, if the gun is small and doesn't allow a shooter's hands to fully grip the gun or pull the trigger properly, it will be difficult for the shooter to control the gun from shot to shot. Another challenge that arises with a gun that doesn't weigh much is the recoil impulse to the hands each time the shooter fires the gun. This may be more than a shooter can endure. It is important that a gun fit the shooter's hands and that the cartridge be chambered in a caliber that he or she is comfortable firing.

This leads to the next consideration: caliber and power rating of the cartridge. The larger the caliber, which relates to the diameter of the bullet, the heavier the bullet. A heavy bullet, comparatively speaking, produces more recoil than a smaller-diameter, lighter bullet. The greater the power rating, which is a combination of the velocity and weight of the bullet fired, the greater the recoil impulse generated. Following Newton's third law, which loosely states that for every action, there is an equal and opposite reaction, an increase in bullet weight and velocity increases the recoil transferred to a shooter's hands. A heavier gun mitigates the recoil impulse a shooter feels, which usually makes it more comfortable to shoot than a lighter gun of a similar size.

It's apparent that the weight of the gun and the power of the cartridge are directly related to a shooter's overall success in making the best selection for the designated application. Compromise is often a necessary factor in finding the best equipment to fulfill the shooter's goal.

SIGHTS

For a marksman, an important consideration in finding the best equipment is the sights.

Sights come in many shapes, sizes and colors. They aid a shooter in achieving the goal of hitting the target. Different shooting disciplines often benefit from specific sight applications to optimize results. How a shooter sees the sights — and uses them for a specific purpose — produces variables that approach the point of infinity.

The sights with which a gun comes equipped are designed to simply help a shooter orient the muzzle to the target. The more specialized the goal, the more specific the sights need to be.

A shooter can experiment with sights in order to optimize the sight picture for the predominant purpose of the gun. Within the realm of reason (and of the rules for competitive shooting), sight selection is a personal choice for a shooter who is at the stage of optimizing equipment. Sights can usually be changed, as the circumstances for their use often vary. A shooter should consider both iron and electronic sights if the objective allows.

TRIGGER

Triggers and trigger mechanisms can be one of the most controversial topics in selecting a gun. Opinions and options abound in every application imaginable.

Regardless of the type of handgun — pistol or revolver — similar types of trigger mechanisms are available to fit a shooter's needs.

A single-action trigger has the hammer or striker precocked, requiring only a simple, short movement of the trigger to release the cocked hammer or striker to fire the gun. The trigger pull is the least resistant and features the shortest pull and reset distances of those available in a handgun.

A double-action-only trigger both cocks and releases the firing mechanism (hammer or striker) with each pull of the trigger. Each trigger pull is the same — from the first shot to the last shot. A double-action-only trigger is available in both revolvers and pistols. The trigger-pull length, reset length and trigger-pull weight are greater in a double-action-only gun than in a single-action gun.

A double-action/single-action trigger has both double-action and single-action capabilities. A semi-automatic pistol with a double-action/single-action trigger usually fires the first shot by cocking and releasing the firing mechanism, after which subsequent shots are fired with a short reset in the single-action mode. A revolver can be fired double-action by simply pulling the trigger; however, the hammer must be manually manipulated in order for the gun to fire single-action.

Each of these trigger types has its advantages and disadvantages depending on the application. There are common factors to all triggers of which a shooter needs to be aware. It must be safe, meaning fully controllable at all times. A trigger should be smooth throughout its full range of motion, and it should be consistent in resistance and movement from start to finish.

Trigger operation is the key to shooting success. A shooter who finds a trigger that suits his or her tastes has a higher likelihood of being successful in any shooting endeavor.

OPERATIONAL VERIFICATION

Although finding the right fit in selecting the best gun for a chosen application is paramount, intrinsic accuracy of the gun is a must to achieve the desired result. The gun, with quality ammunition, should be able to shoot as well and preferably better than the person shooting it. If a shooter intends to use the gun for target-shooting purposes, it should be mechanically capable of shooting a shot group equal to a perfect score, or smaller, consistently, using target ammunition commensurate with the discipline being shot.

A shooter can verify mechanical accuracy of a gun and ammunition by firing the gun in a machine rest or from a bench rest at the maximum distance from which the pistol will be used.

Having a gun and ammunition that will shoot at this level is important since it builds realistic expectations in a shooter's skill and capability. It does this by eliminating the excuse of "equipment failure" that many people blame for poor performance. If the gun will shoot a perfect score mechanically and the shooter's performance doesn't meet that level of proficiency, it is hard to put the blame where it is not warranted.

A serious shooter will verify both gun and ammunition performance periodically. Factory ammunition is made in lots, as is remanufactured and sometimes even reloaded ammunition. It is common for different lots of ammunition to have different levels of performance in a single gun. This makes it important for a shooter — especially one who has changed lots of ammunition — to validate each lot's performance prior to practice or competition. This will eliminate any doubt regarding performance of the shooter's equipment.

Having good equipment helps a shooter focus on correcting performance deficiencies where they exist instead of placing the blame in an area undeserving of that scrutiny.

ADDITIONAL ACCESSORIES

Once a shooter has a handgun, ammunition and safety gear in place, it is time to add the accessories that will support the chosen application. This can be a daunting task simply because of all of the available options.

Usually, having a means of transporting guns and ammo to the range is a logical approach. A range bag with multiple compartments for accessories is a good starting point. The range bag should have a padded compartment to protect the gun and separate compartments for items such as:

- Boxes of ammunition
- Safety gear
- Cleaning equipment
- Lubricant
- Holsters
- Magazine pouches
- Speedloader holders
- A small tool kit
- A first-aid kit
- Lens cleaner
- A notebook
- Writing utensils
- A water bottle
- Additional items a shooter desires

The choices and options are infinite and will likely change over time as the shooter's habits become more regimented.

STREAMLINING SUCCESS

The quest for good equipment does not need to be a continuous buying spree. In fact, buying and having a lot of equipment and not knowing how to use it is counterproductive. Money spent on training might be a better path to success — provided the shooter's equipment is on par with his or her ability to use it. That said, without equipment that matches or exceeds a shooter's capability, the best level of performance is unlikely to come to fruition.

Regardless of a serious shooter's chosen application or discipline, good equipment streamlines the road to success.

CHAPTER 11

DIAGNOSTICS AND TROUBLESHOOTING

Every shooter — regardless of shooting application or chosen discipline — experiences the highs and lows of shooting performance. The ability to diagnose shooting deficiencies is essential in starting the process of troubleshooting and repairing the error in the shot-delivery process.

In many cases, a shooter needs a shooting instructor, a coach or another shooter to identify the deficiency and provide material to remedy the problem. However, with experience, a seasoned shooter can develop the ability to detect and correct problems without the assistance of others. That said, it is usually good to get a second opinion from a trusted authority to ensure and validate that the issue has been thoroughly examined and addressed.

In either case, the concern must first be identified and isolated. Keep in mind that there may be multiple deficiencies causing the problem.

By following a simple formula, a shooter can diagnose and correct most shooting problems in short order. It is important to be specific — with as much detail as possible — to identify the root cause of the problem.

The first step is to determine what the problem is. Once a shooter has determined what the problem actually is, the question of why the problem exists becomes the next step in correcting it. The third step toward achieving progress is deciding how to go about fixing and eliminating the deficiency for good.

Identifying what the problem is, why the shooter is doing it and how to fix it can be made a little easier by breaking down shooting performance into these three categories: visual, biomechanical and mental. They are the three predominant areas from which shooting performance originates. Sometimes the performance deficiency occurs in one of these three areas, but, more often than not, it is a combination of two or three that must be analyzed and remedied.

Many times, a shooter can achieve the quickest result by taking a holistic approach and looking at vision, biomechanics and the brain together to determine what is necessary to achieve success. Understanding how they interact with one another to deliver a shot or series of shots comes with experience, but realizing how to use natural attributes such as peripheral vision, eye-hand coordination, and how the brain processes and stores information is a good start.

The compilation of diagnostic and troubleshooting tools presented here comes from decades of working with shooters from many different backgrounds around the world. It includes what has worked for me and my colleagues most often and what we have found most prevalent among students. The material is easy to understand, convey and perform.

INVOLUNTARY MOVEMENT

One of the most common problems encountered by a shooter is involuntarily adding movement to the gun while pulling the trigger. This movement can be associated with flinching, anticipating the recoil, jerking the trigger, heeling and other factors the shooter uses to blame the muzzle for not being stabilized on the target when the bullet exits, resulting in an undesirable shot.

The two most important diagnostic and prevention exercises to control involuntary movement while shooting

are the "Noise Inoculation Drill" and the "Recoil Inoculation Drill." These drills are rarely used but are essential in laying a good foundation for shooting any type of firearm. Students and firearms instructors rarely have any knowledge or experience with these exercises.

The basis of these two inoculation drills originates from an individual's natural response to an unexpected or unfamiliar loud noise and the unfamiliar and perceptually uncontrolled movement of an object moving toward the eyes (in close proximity to the face). When either or both conditions take place, the typical result for a shooter is an involuntary movement, often referred to as a "flinch." This quickly transforms into an anticipatory action of trigger and firearm movement immediately prior to releasing the shot, resulting in an unsatisfactory hit.

Understanding what causes the mental and physical responses of involuntary movement — flinching, anticipating or what could be called a "self-preservation response" while shooting or in the presence of gunfire — is necessary to ultimately fix the problem.

Flinching or anticipating a gun's firing is a condition that materializes from the subconscious mind. It is a physical response to an event that is perceived as unpleasant and possibly dangerous to a shooter's physical well-being. When associated with a firearm, it is stimulated by the loud noise of discharge and the seemingly uncontrollable movement of a hand-held object in the space close in proximity to a shooter's head and eyes.

The physical response is usually exemplified by the shooter closing his or her eyes prior to or while pulling the trigger, concurrently pushing the gun away from the head and eyes, preempting the movement of the gun during recoil. This action almost always moves the muzzle of the gun off the target. The result drastically decreases the likelihood of a successful hit on the target.

The reason for this phenomenon is rooted in the crisis-control center of the brain (the "amygdala").

Take a moment to think about how you would react if an unexpected loud noise were to occur while you were quietly reading a book. Your train of thought would be broken, you would momentarily close your eyes, you would move involuntarily by tensing your muscles, and, most likely, you would move to escape what you perceived to be a threat. This is largely what happens when a flinch takes place.

Conventional training suggests that someone who shoots enough, perhaps thousands of rounds, will eventually overcome the flinch phenomenon. This may be true, but the noise and recoil inoculation drills are a better means — requiring less time and ammunition — of overcoming this innate self-preservation response.

It is important for a shooter, regardless of experience level, to understand why the sound of a gun and the movement (recoil) of a gun in the visual field would be objectionable.

Since the average human can process, under the best of circumstances, five to seven bits of information simultaneously in the conscious mind, it stands to reason that as a person's stress level increases, the number of information bits that can be processed decreases. This varies from person to person, but typical results show that a shooter processes only two to three bits of information when working with firearms because of the perceived gravity and danger of the situation.

In conventional firearms training, students are taught stance, grip responsibilities, breathing, sight alignment, sight picture and trigger control, among other things. There is no room in a shooter's conscious mind to process all of this information, much less worry about what the gun sounds like or how it moves during recoil.

Since the subconscious mind downloads information of this type by way of the conscious mind, there is little chance that a shooter's subconscious has received the message that the noise and movement of the gun is of no consequence to the physical well-being of the rest of the body.

Understanding how the brain learns and responds to threatening situations is essential to successfully eliminating fear of the gun and controlling the self-preservation response. The next step is practical application on the range.

LISTENING TO AND FEELING THE GUN

The "Noise Inoculation Drill" allows a shooter to focus on gun noise, with a secondary awareness of a gun's movement.

The first step is for the shooter to assume a comfortable shooting position, point the gun into a suitable backstop with no target, and dry-fire the gun (with eyes closed). Closing the eyes will allow the shooter to focus primarily on hearing and touch, which are the two areas of interest in this exercise.

After completing several repetitions dry, the shooter can, with the addition of eye and ear protection, fire the gun into a safe backstop with live ammunition. The shooter will fire a single shot at a time, on command, while being supervised by an instructor or coach.

The shooter's initial focus should be on the sound of the gun, listening to and savoring each individual shot until comfortable with the sound of the firearm. This assures the amygdala that this sound is of no consequence to the shooter's personal safety; therefore, there is no reason for alarm when this sound occurs.

The goal of the "Recoil Inoculation Drill" is for the shooter to feel the push of the gun in the hands as the muzzle lifts and settles with each shot fired. The shooter's eyes are still closed in this step. The objective is to listen to the sound of the gun and feel the movement of the gun — without additional sensory input — during the trigger pull.

The shooter should be permitted to shoot, with supervision, until he or she is comfortable with the sound and feel of the gun when it fires. Although there shouldn't be a set limit to the number of shots for the shooter to achieve a state of feeling comfortable, five to six shots for each of the two steps is often adequate for someone who needs to accomplish the task of eliminating the fear of the sound and movement of a gun.

Building on hearing the gun and feeling the push of the gun in the hands, the third step focuses on the shooter seeing the gun's actual movement when it fires. This step allows the shooter to watch the gun's movement from either side and then from the rear. The shooter is focusing on how little the gun actually moves in a two-handed hold. As before, it is important to allow as many shots as necessary to show the shooter that the gun's movement and noise are of no consequence to his or her personal safety. In fact, it is beneficial for the instructor or coach to suggest that the experience of the noise and recoil inoculation drills is an empowering event, enabling the shooter to control an object of such power without fear.

These three steps allow a shooter to assure the subconscious mind, through the cognitive download of practical experience, that the sound and the movement of the gun when it fires won't cause any personal harm.

At this juncture, there is no reason for the shooter to fear the gun and little incentive to flinch when firing it in the future. In fact, the shooter may start to see things that previously went unnoticed. This may include brass exiting the ejection port or smoke and flash at the muzzle around the front sight when it is in focus at the moment of discharge. These are major contributors to improving shooter performance.

On occasion, a shooter, typically an experienced one, may have to perform the "Noise Inoculation Drill" or the "Recoil Inoculation Drill" — or both — to break deeply ingrained habits that sometimes surface as involuntary movement. Reinforcing good habits will suppress the bad ones and eventually make them a thing of the past.

TRIGGER JERK

The trigger jerk is often associated with flinch but has other causes aside from the uncertainty and fear of what is taking place close to a shooter's face. Sometimes trigger jerk is a means to hurry up and get past the unpleasantries of the noise and recoil of the gun. It is not uncommon for a shooter to flinch and then jerk the trigger in quick succession, neither of which will contribute to hitting the target.

The inoculation drills just mentioned will help eliminate this type of trigger jerk as well as the flinch.

Trigger jerk can also be caused by the visual perception of the sight picture. The sight picture is the relationship of the correctly aligned sights on the gun to the target the shooter is engaging.

When using iron sights for precision shooting, a shooter obtains the best results with a hard visual focus on the front sight, viewed through the opening in the rear sight, superimposed on the center of the target. If the shooter's eye focus transitions past the front sight, toward the target, the perceived movement of the gun on the target increases. The closer the eye focus to the target, the greater the apparent movement of the gun in relation to the target. This increased movement makes the shooter anxious to take the shot, which causes a jerk of the trigger before the perceived movement gets any worse.

It is not uncommon for a gun to remain stable on the target until the shooter starts to pull the trigger. Once that happens, the gun's stability on the target ceases to be at an acceptable level. If an instructor or fellow shooter were to ask the offender to identify where eye focus was concentrated when the shot broke, the shooter wouldn't be able to say. One thing for sure is that the shooter's eye focus wasn't on the front sight.

Sometimes a shooter wants to see perfect sight alignment first and then the perceived perfect sight picture. The individual will check and recheck both the sight alignment and the sight picture multiple times and eventually run out of patience, oxygen in the lungs or time, which results in a trigger jerk to make the gun fire. The shooter will then move on to the next shot in the sequence. Again, a shooter who is being honest will unlikely be able to tell where the sights were in relation to the target when the bullet left the barrel.

There are multiple ways to diagnose and cure a shooter who jerks the trigger because of visual information fed to the brain.

It is best to first establish that the shooter's eyes are open when the shot or shots are fired. Even if the shooter has performed the noise and recoil inoculation drills, a deep-seated habit of blinking the eyes at the moment of discharge may still occur. This condition is prevalent with experienced shooters who have a number of bad habits they are working to overcome. If fear of noise and recoil are not concerns, then logic and reason can be used to create an expectation of what the shooter should be seeing for best performance.

It has already been established that a shooter's eye focus should be on the front sight — with a secondary awareness of the rear sight — at the moment of discharge.

By directing a shooter's attention to where the ejection port is located (between the front and rear sights) and confirming what exits the ejection port every time the gun fires (the spent cartridge case), logic dictates that if the shooter's eyes are open when the gun fires, the spent cartridge case will be, at a minimum, peripherally visible as it ejects from the ejection port.

It is an indisputable fact that a spent cartridge case exits the ejection port every time the gun fires. If the shooter does

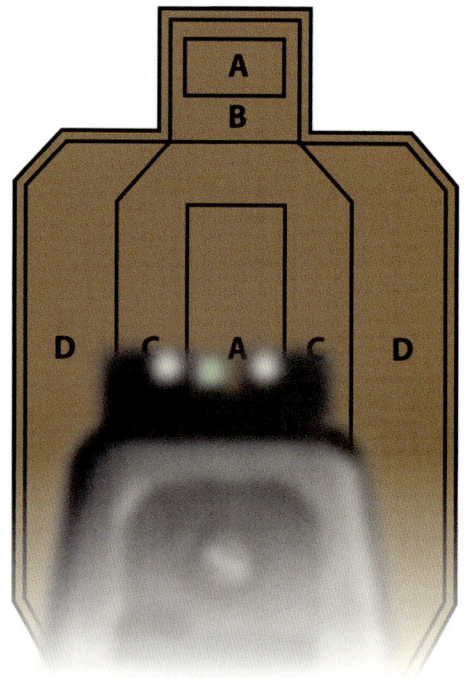

not see any ejected cases, the eyes are most likely closed. Looking at it logically, a shooter who is allowed to fire into a safe backstop while focusing primarily on the ejection port will begin to recognize the ejected cartridges as the eyes remain open during the shooting process.

Once it is established that the shooter's eyes are open during firing, where the eyes are focused at the moment of discharge must be confirmed next.

Again, logic can be used to help determine where the shooter's eyes are focused before, during and after the shot. It is important for an instructor or coach to confirm with the shooter what takes place at the muzzle, from a visual perspective, each time the gun fires.

Another indisputable fact is that smoke and flash exit and appear at the muzzle when the bullet clears the barrel on its way to the target. Since the front sight is only a fraction of an inch above the muzzle, it stands to reason that the atmospheric disturbance at the muzzle that takes place when the bullet exits will be visible to the shooter if the eyes are focused on the front sight. If the shooter is not seeing the smoke and flash at the muzzle on a consistent basis, the eyes are shut when the gun fires (or eye focus has transitioned past the gun, toward the target, prior to the bullet exiting the muzzle). In order to properly follow through on each shot, the shooter's eye focus must be on the front sight — with the muzzle stabilized on the target until the bullet exits the muzzle — which is determined by seeing the smoke and flash at the muzzle.

Remember, the shooter has total control of where the bullet will go until the bullet exits the barrel. Once the bullet has cleared contact with the barrel, the shooter no longer has influence on its trajectory to the target.

It should also be mentioned that when the shooter's eye focus is on the sights superimposed on the target, calling the placement of the hits on the target becomes much easier.

Training the eye to stay on the front sight in order to recognize the visual cues of smoke and blast is sometimes necessary for a shooter to experience consistency in visual performance.

WALL DRILL

The "Wall Drill" was first designed to prevent focus creep past the front sight as a shooter pulls the trigger. When done correctly, it forces the shooter's eye to stay focused on the front sight through the rear-sight opening until the hammer falls or the striker releases as the individual pulls the trigger.

To recap from previous chapters, the "Wall Drill" is performed dry, in a safe environment, from the normal shooting position and with the muzzle in contact or slightly clear of a blank vertical surface, such as a wall.

The gun is empty not only for safety's sake but also to show any deficiencies in the shooter's grip or muzzle stability during trigger manipulation, which may be masked when firing live ammunition. The vertical surface blocks the vision from transitioning forward of the gun and trains the eye to stay open and focused on the front sight through the release of the trigger, ensuring follow-through. It is important that the vertical surface have no distracting features, which will interfere with full attention of the eye on the front sight.

Practicing the "Wall Drill" is a simple and easy process:

1. After verifying the gun as clear and empty, cock the hammer or set the firing mechanism in the ready-to-fire condition.

2. Assume a comfortable shooting position, with the muzzle in light contact with the wall or another suitable vertical surface.

3. Focus the eye or eyes on the front sight as it appears through the window of the rear-sight opening.

4. Contact the trigger with the trigger finger and apply pressure until the hammer falls or the firing mechanism is released.

5. Repeat several times, taking note of any movement of the front sight in the window of the rear-sight opening or any movement induced into the gun by the grip or trigger-finger movement when the shot is released.

3N1 DRILL

Coupled with the "Wall Drill," the "3N1 Drill" will coordinate and direct the three critical components of shot delivery to achieve optimal and consistent results. This drill is best learned with dry repetition at the wall and then transitioned to live-fire once a shooter can perform the drill on demand with little to no conscious thought. The drill integrates visual focus on the sights and the physical act of trigger manipulation into a single mental exercise.

To perform the "3N1 Drill," the shooter must pull the trigger while applying maximum visual focus on the front sight through the window of the rear-sight opening, mentally envisioning a physical connection between the two. The mental image of the trigger pulling the centered front sight through the rear-sight opening to release the shot ensures active coordination between the eye, brain and trigger finger for every shot fired.

This drill combines the three components of shot delivery — mental, visual and physical — with equal priority.

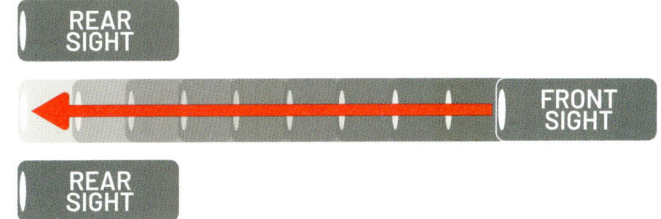

Concentration on pulling the front sight with the trigger while keeping it centered in the rear-sight opening serves to perfect trigger movement and sight alignment simultaneously. It also eliminates mental distractions. This is because both actions occupy the shooter's mental focus with the essential elements necessary to execute the best shot possible.

BALL AND DUMMY DRILL

Another way of diagnosing involuntary and unwanted movement of the gun while pulling the trigger is the age-old "Ball and Dummy Drill." Mixing dummy and live rounds in the shooter's gun often reveals that during trigger movement, unnecessary movement takes place at the muzzle. Of course, this would result in an undesirable shot if the dummy round were live. The goal is for the shooter to condition the trigger finger to move the trigger past the threshold of firing the gun without influencing the muzzle's relationship to the target.

The drill is particularly effective when an individual is firing multiple shots at an elevated rate of speed, where the shooter's haste in firing overcomes the need to smoothly manipulate the trigger for peak accuracy.

Similarly, a shooter can combine the "Ball and Dummy Drill" with immediate-action drills, where, when the gun fails to fire, he or she performs immediate action to restore the gun's ability to fire.

A shooter's visual performance can be measured with the "Ball and Dummy Drill" by bringing to light poor trigger operation, which results in unintended movement of the muzzle on the target. If the shooter fails to recognize the muzzle's errant movement, it becomes obvious that the eyes are shut or focused elsewhere at the moment of discharge.

If the shooter does recognize a dip in the muzzle or other movement of the gun while pulling the trigger, it is a sign that the movement is regularly taking place — without realization — but is masked by the gun's recoil when the gun fires.

Smooth operation of the trigger is essential for the best levels of accuracy. Practicing the "Wall Drill" to achieve an acceptable trigger pull with single and multiple shots will usually remedy the problem.

It is important to remember that with these and other exercises designed to optimize a shooter's marksmanship ability, the goal is to stabilize the muzzle on the target long enough for the bullet to exit without being influenced by the movement of the trigger. This is true regardless of how quickly or slowly the shooter fires.

When a shooter is having difficulty putting consistent hits on target and dummy rounds are not available to perform the "Ball and Dummy Drill," there are several drills that can be self-administered to diagnose the deficiency.

FIVE-AND-FIVE DRILL

The "Five-and-Five Drill" is a simple and effective way to detect and correct intermittent errors in controlling the trigger.

The drill consists of loading and firing five live rounds at a speed determined by the shooter, immediately followed by firing five dry shots in sequence with the live shots (for a total of 10 consecutive trigger pulls). If there are deficiencies that need to be corrected in operating the trigger, they will become apparent in the five dry cycles of the trigger. Any movement of the muzzle during the dry shots will correspond to the placement of the shots on target during the five live shots.

Practicing the "Wall Drill" will help a shooter condition the trigger finger to operate the trigger smoothly and without adding motion to the gun.

DOUBLE-ACTION TO SINGLE-ACTION TRANSITION DRILL

The "Double-Action to Single-Action Transition Drill" was developed to diagnose and correct the inability of a shooter equipped with a double-action-first-shot/single-action-follow-up-shot pistol, such as the Beretta 92 or the SIG Sauer P226, to place the double-action shots and the single-action shots with any degree of accuracy on the target.

Some originally thought that the first shot out of the pistol, which was fired double-action, was little more than a throwaway shot because of the longer and heavier pull of the trigger. Once that shot was fired, the gun then transitioned to single-action mode, with the lighter and shorter trigger pull, making the gun easier to shoot. This belief was so strong that some instructors actually taught their students to shoot the first round into the ground and then carry on with the rest of their shots in single-action. Other instructors considered this practice dangerous and legally imprudent. Because of this, they sought to find a better answer to the perceived problem.

It didn't take long for these instructors to discover that of the first two shots fired, the first shot, fired in double-action, was the shot that hit the mark and, in fact, the second shot fired in single-action was the errant shot. Further study showed that a shooter often felt impaired by the perceived length of time to pull the trigger, cocking and releasing the hammer in double-action to fire the first shot — so much so that the shooter had to hurry the single-action second shot because he or she lacked confidence that the first shot could be effective. What was observed and confirmed was that the shooter, in the haste of firing the second shot, pulled the trigger in such a manner as to move the muzzle of the gun off the target. This concept was hard to sell to many who were teaching and practicing that the first shot out of a double-action/single-action pistol was dubious in the arena of accuracy.

In order to prove the point that the double-action shot was likely the one that hit the target as opposed to the single-action-follow-up shot, the "Double-Action to Single-Action Transition Drill" was developed. It was simple and effective in proving a point and improved a shooter's hits on target.

To start the drill, the shooter must chamber a round from the magazine, remove the magazine, leave one round in the gun, decock and holster or come to the ready position. On the signal to fire, the shooter engages the target with two pulls of the trigger: one live-fire and one dry-fire. Repeating this sequence several times usually shows that when the hammer falls for the second time, the muzzle moves excessively, caused by how the shooter pulls the trigger. The learning point is that the shooter must pull the trigger in such a manner as to not move the muzzle off the target, regardless of whether that happens in double-action or single-action.

If a shooter fails to fire the first two shots out of a double-action/single-action pistol with sufficient accuracy, practicing the "Double-Action to Single-Action Transition Drill" will help to both detect and correct the deficiency.

This is also a good drill for a shooter who is unable to fire two shots in sequence with satisfactory accuracy. The lesson in this case is that the shooter needs to have patience to smoothly move the trigger every time so as not to affect the muzzle's position on the target. Consciously feeling the trigger movement is critical.

Practicing the "Wall Drill" will aid in conditioning a shooter's index finger to move smoothly when the shooter is dry-firing. Practicing the "3N1 Drill" will condition the trigger finger to move smoothly and deliberately when the shooter is firing live ammunition. Diagnosing and correcting deficiencies in a shooter's ability to fire all shots accurately from a double-action/single-action handgun all lead back to the same tenets of handgun marksmanship: to stabilize the muzzle on the target and operate the trigger without affecting the muzzle's relationship to the target.

VALIDATING FRONT-SIGHT FOCUS

After all of the practicing and being preached to, a shooter might start to lose hard focus on the front sight without consciously being aware of it. This results in several signs shown by the hits on the target. With a shooter's soft focus on the sights, groups start to get larger and evolve to a vertical spread from the intended hit location to points significantly lower. This vertical stringing is the result of the aiming eye inconsistently focusing on any plane from the front sight to the target. This can easily be verified by an instructor, a coach or another shooter standing safely to the side and observing the pupil of the shooter's aiming eye.

CHAMBER A ROUND FROM THE MAGAZINE.

REMOVE THE MAGAZINE, LEAVING ONE ROUND IN THE GUN.

DECOCK AND HOLSTER OR COME TO THE READY POSITION.

ON THE SIGNAL TO FIRE, ENGAGE THE TARGET WITH TWO PULLS OF THE TRIGGER: ONE LIVE-FIRE AND ONE DRY-FIRE.

5 YARDS **10 YARDS** **15 YARDS**

As the eye focus transitions from the gun to the target and back again, the pupil will expand and contract to accommodate the focus accordingly. The observer should notice the gun moving up and down slightly, in concert with the eye focus changes. This is because as the shooter takes a peek at the target, he or she has to slightly lower the gun to see the target. When the eye focus is brought back to the sights, the gun has to be raised slightly to see the correct sight picture with the sights on the target. The fact that the gun may fire at any point during this sequence results in vertical stringing of hits on the target.

Another similar but not identical phenomenon is when a shooter fires acceptable groups at the point of aim on a target that is relatively close but starts to hit lower on the target than the intended point of impact as distance increases, usually past 10 yards. The impacts become increasingly lower on the target as the distance increases until the shooter misses the target entirely.

This is a classic case of the shooter looking over the sights at the target to see where the bullet is going to impact before firing the shot. This can happen because the shooter wishes to see where the bullets are hitting or because of lack of patience to let the bullet clear the muzzle before shifting eye focus downrange. The shooter likely lacks confidence in his or her shooting ability and therefore wants to see whether or not the bullets are hitting the target.

A shooter who can fire good groups at shorter distances possesses an acceptable level of shot-delivery mechanics. If the problem is firing at distance, where the shooter is pointing the muzzle (instead of where the eyes are focused) during firing is the problem.

In some cases, revisiting the exercise where a shooter recognizes the smoke and flash surrounding the front sight as the bullet exits the muzzle — as well as having a peripheral awareness of the spent cartridge as it ejects from the ejection port — will keep the muzzle in the proper position for the shooter to hit the target from multiple distances. This will ensure that the shooter's eye focus is on the gun, looking at the sights, instead of on the target looking over the sights.

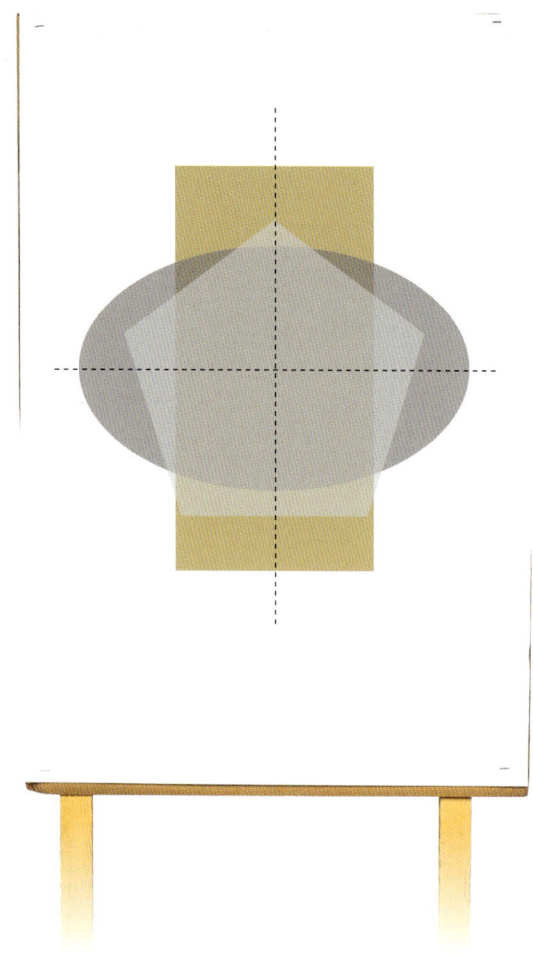

SHOOT THE SHAPE DRILL

In an extreme case, where a shooter insists on looking at the target to verify the position of the sights on the target (or for reasons previously mentioned), firing at a blank target with nothing specific at which to aim will aid that shooter in properly managing the muzzle. This ensures the shots will impact the center of the target up close or at the maximum effective range of the handgun — or anywhere in between. The eye's natural ability to define center, no matter the shape, will consistently put the shots where they need to be: centered on the object.

It's as simple as aligning the sights on what the shooter perceives as the center of the target, regardless of its size or shape, and pulling the trigger — all while keeping eye focus on the sights until the shooter observes the smoke and flash. Holding the sights in the center of the target and pulling the trigger several times in sequence using this technique, without looking for the impacts on the target, will result in a very pleasant surprise of closely grouped shots. By simplifying the target to a shape at which to aim rather than a specific spot on a target, the shooter can concentrate on the sights and control the trigger without distraction, which is where accurate shooting originates. The added benefit of putting the sights on the center of the target, regardless of the shape or size of the target, is that center hits on the target will occur.

SIMPLIFIED SIGHT PICTURE

Added to the concept of shooting the center of the shape is a simplified sight picture. This sight picture makes shooting and hitting the center of a target even easier because of how the sights are viewed in relation to the target.

The simplified sight picture is referred to as "float the dot and shoot the shot."

The phrase describes what the shooter sees as he or she pulls the trigger to shoot an accurate shot.

The dot refers to the painted dot or night sight embedded into the face of the front sight. When looking at and focusing on the center of the dot through the opening in the rear sight, the eye will visually align the two sights automatically. This eliminates the need to check the perimeter of the front sight constantly to verify where it is positioned in the rear-sight opening. This automatic alignment saves time and minimizes eye strain when a shooter is fine-tuning the muzzle's position on the target. By combining the aforementioned sight picture with the concept of shooting at the center of whatever the target may be, the shooter simplifies the whole process of shooting an accurate shot or series of shots. Ultimately, the problem of shooting lower on the target as distance increases is eliminated when a shooter floats the front-sight dot in the center of the target while pulling the trigger to fire the shot. It is less tempting to look over the gun toward the target when using this technique because the shooter knows the shot will hit where the dot is located on the target the moment the gun fires.

An additional benefit gained with this concept is a shooter's acceptance of natural gun movement when trying to stabilize the muzzle on the target. It is a physiological fact that being perfectly still without support is impossible. In allowing the front-sight dot to "float" on the center of the target — like a beach ball floating on a pond in a gentle breeze — the shooter learns to accept the inevitable gun movement without negative effect.

CORRECTING GRIP DEFICIENCIES

Diagnosing flaws in a shooter's grip and correcting the deficiencies may require multiple approaches.

First, it is important to define what is necessary to attain a satisfactory grip on a handgun. The variables in gun size, weight and caliber among all of the brands available are nearly infinite. Add to that the size and strength of the shooter's hands as well as palm size and finger lengths. These mechanical and physiological variables make it necessary to identify some guidelines before isolating and correcting any issues.

"FLOAT THE DOT, SHOOT THE SHOT."

If possible, fit the gun to the shooter, seating the grip of the gun in the web of the shooter's hand — between the thumb and index finger — so that the extended index finger of the primary shooting hand and the barrel of the gun point in the same general direction. The index finger should be able to make full contact across the face of the trigger in order to apply pressure through the pull — in line with the frame — to fire the gun. A shooter being able to point the muzzle where the eye is looking and to pull the trigger without adding motion to the gun is indicative of an optimal hand-to-handgun fit.

A shooter may be provided with a gun or own one that isn't a perfect fit. In most cases, there is a degree of adaptability between the shooter and the gun.

There are several guidelines to follow that will determine whether the shooter's gun and grip are compatible.

To obtain his or her best performance, a shooter must be able to consistently hold the gun on a target with one or both hands and pull the trigger without adding extra motion to the gun or moving the muzzle off the target. These are basic tenets of marksmanship and will help validate that the size of the gun is workable for the shooter.

Consistency in controlling the movement of the gun during firing is an important factor for a shooter to define and apply. Contrary to the popular belief that all the pressure a shooter can muster is the best way to control gun movement, there is a better way to achieve success. Besides, how long can a person exert maximum pressure before the pressure and therefore the consistency diminish in the effort?

The amount of pressure necessary may vary with gun type and caliber, but it can be defined as the amount of pressure necessary to prevent the gun from slipping in the hands for a single shot or during a series of shots. Maximum friction via contact between the surfaces of the hands and the grip of the gun, combined with moderate grip pressure, will prevent the gun from shifting in the hands when the shooter fires. Allowing the gun to rise and settle naturally, without fighting the recoil, easily facilitates this concept and is in fact a more efficient method for firing multiple shots. Consistent grip pressure combined with maximum friction on the grip surfaces of the gun is a foundational factor in placing each shot in the desired location.

It is possible to grip the gun too much — so much so that it degrades shooting performance. As mentioned previously, sustaining maximum pressure for any length of time is impossible and leads to inconsistency, which is detrimental to the overall outcome. When a shooter is exerting maximum pressure on the grip of a gun, the skin on the surface of the hands will tend to wrinkle, decreasing contact and therefore reducing the friction factor between the two.

This is sometimes hard to diagnose, but relaxing the grip slightly and concentrating on pulling the trigger parallel to the frame will almost always improve shooting performance. As long as the gun does not slip in a shooter's hands during firing, the applied pressure is sufficient to control and guide the gun.

Gripping the gun too tightly regularly restricts the range of motion of the trigger finger, making it difficult to fully pull the trigger. When the shooter runs out of patience or oxygen (due to the inability to fire the gun without jerking the trigger) and decides to abort the shot, if the trigger finger is on the trigger the moment

the shooter relaxes the grip, that finger is freed up to move the additional distance required to fire the gun. Anytime a shooter consciously changes grip pressure, the trigger finger should be off the trigger to prevent an inadvertent discharge.

Sometimes, the grip deficiency comes as a product of pulling the trigger. This combination often masks the real problem and can lead to a partial or false diagnosis.

An example would be a right-handed shooter firing groups that are good but that are all low and to the left of the desired point of impact. (For a left-handed shooter, the groups would print low and to the right.) Since the groups were acceptable, it would stand to reason that adjusting the sights would fix the problem. Should the sight adjustment fail to fix the problem, a shooter can take several steps to narrow down and correct the cause of the misplaced group of shots.

The easiest and most simple technique is for the shooter to shoot the gun with the other hand and see where the groups print. Typically, the groups will change location, even with the original sight setting. This indicates that the shooter is inducing the change in impact by how he or she is holding the gun while shooting it. In the rare instance that the groups impact in the same location when the shooter uses either hand and refuses to move appreciably with an adjustment of the sights, there is a mechanical problem with the gun that has to be dealt with before further action can be taken.

THREE-HAND DRILL

If it is determined that the shooter is at fault, diagnosing the cause can be as simple as having the shooter hold the gun on the target — using the normal grip and sight picture — without touching the trigger. Then an

instructor or coach should place his or her hand over the shooter's hand and pull the trigger to fire the shot. Without the influence of the shooter's trigger finger, the shots should impact in the desired location with the sights correctly adjusted. In essence, this proves the shooter is gripping the gun with such force that when the trigger finger increases pressure on the trigger, the rest of the fingers increase pressure on the grip, causing the gun to rotate slightly down and laterally away from the point of aim. Loosening the grip on the gun to give the trigger finger the ability to move independently, without restriction, will allow the sights and muzzle to stay on the target as the bullet exits the muzzle.

LIMP WRISTING

Another phenomenon that is often linked to gripping a handgun is referred to as "limp wristing." This is described as a failure of the shooter to sufficiently support the frame of a semi-automatic pistol in the hands to allow the slide to cycle through extracting or ejecting the fired cartridge. Limp wristing is a controversial subject that may result from the ammunition being fired, the firearm itself, the shooter or a combination of all of them.

The diagnosis for the shooter can usually be determined by performing the "Ball and Dummy Drill." The first step is to observe for errant movement in the gun as the shooter pulls the trigger. If the movement is present and can't be controlled and eliminated, revisiting the "Noise Inoculation Drill" and the "Recoil Inoculation Drill" will help the shooter to pull the trigger while consistently maintaining muzzle stability on the target. Revisiting the "Wall Drill" will help to reestablish the foundational mechanics of pulling the trigger on demand without affecting the rest of the gun.

Limp wristing can be caused by or exacerbated by an improperly maintained pistol. A simple cleaning, inspection, lubrication and function check may solve and eliminate the problem altogether.

Weak ammunition can also be the culprit in a semi-automatic pistol's failure to complete the operating cycle. Changing to factory-fresh Sporting Arms and Ammunition Manufacturers' Institute-rated or military-rated ammunition will ensure that the ammunition has adequate power to cycle a properly functioning firearm. It is prudent to fire both practice- and service-grade ammunition to validate compatibility with the pistol.

Videotaping a shooter and slowing down the speed of the video is a good means of discovering any shooter-induced failures in the firearm. Sometimes it's necessary in order to diagnose the failure of a shooter to execute good shooting practices.

So-called "limp wristing" can be effectively eliminated by exploring one or all of these avenues to detect and correct a shooter's root problem.

STABILIZING THE MUZZLE

Stabilizing the muzzle on the target is one of the basic components of handgun marksmanship. An easy way to diagnose and determine a shooter's ability to hold on a target with minimal muzzle movement is to use a laser mounted to the gun when the shooter is practicing dry-fire exercises. It is particularly effective at the maximum distances the shooter is likely to encounter. A shooter can use different grip pressures and body positions to optimize balance, which will enhance the stability of the laser and therefore the muzzle on the target. Eliminating as much body tension as possible will help the shooter subdue movement as well.

Once the hold on the target is satisfactorily stable, the shooter can add the next component of precision marksmanship to the equation. The desired goal is for the shooter to pull the trigger on the unloaded handgun — replicating firing the shot — without affecting the laser's movement on the target. Keep in mind that the laser will always be moving. The shooter's goal is to pull the trigger without increasing the degree of movement. It is beneficial for the shooter to practice operating the

trigger from every position and in every condition used in live-fire. This exercise will help to perfect a shooter's grip pressure and trigger-finger movement whenever he or she fires a shot or shots. Combining hold control and trigger control with a laser in dry practice will validate the capabilities of a shooter to perform the two foundational skills of muzzle management and trigger-finger discipline necessary to fire a gun with accuracy.

A laser also helps in evaluating how well a shooter is using the metallic sights on a gun. The shooter should fire several groups using the iron sights — at or near the maximum distance at which the gun will be used — and then fire groups at the same distance using the laser only. If the groups are better with the laser, it indicates that there is room for the shooter to improve using the conventional sights on the gun. Ideally, the groups will be comparable, indicating that the shooter is delivering the best performance possible with the applicable equipment.

The same diagnostic can be used with a red-dot sight or other type of optic to verify a shooter's capability with each method of aiming.

VISION ANOMALIES

A shooter who claims vision difficulties as being the source of her or her shooting woes should begin the process of correction and improvement by first verifying eye dominance. In addition to the method described in Chapter 6, a shooter can determine eye dominance by looking at an object across the room, covering the viewed image with the thumb of the dominant hand, and closing or occluding one eye, then the other. The eye seeing the thumb and the object in alignment is the dominant eye. The non-dominant eye sees the thumb misaligned and off to one side. Ideally, for a shooter, the dominant eye and the dominant hand correspond. Having the dominant eye and dominant hand on the same side of the body makes it easier for the shooter to fire with both eyes open, which simplifies acquiring the sight alignment and sight picture necessary to hit the intended target.

After establishing which eye is dominant, a shooter can undertake further measures to improve the visual input necessary to shoot accurately.

A shooter whose dominant eye does not correspond with the dominant hand is considered "cross-dominant." As such, the shooter has several paths that will help enable shooting to his or her full potential. This will require some modification in the use of the hands, eyes or both.

For a novice shooter, learning to shoot with the hand that corresponds with the dominant eye will simplify the shooting goals. This applies particularly to shotguns and rifles and less so to handguns.

For a shooter who is unable or unwilling to switch the shooting hand to correspond with the dominant eye, there are multiple options to correct the problem. Some incorporate visual aids, which are useful only on the range when an individual is shooting informally or in specific types of competition, where the shooter can enhance performance. Others enable the shooter to adapt the shooting technique to the conditions presented with only what's always available.

An easy fix is for the shooter to shoot with the dominant hand and close or squint the dominant eye while aiming with the non-dominant eye. For the rare individual who cannot close or squint the dominant eye, turning the head slightly and then aligning the dominant eye with the sights and the target presents a viable option. Either of these options performed consistently will yield excellent results for the cross-dominant handgun shooter — without aids to block the visual input to the dominant eye.

A competitive shooter firing from a stationary position sometimes finds that limiting visual information entering the non-aiming eye while maintaining the same light level for both eyes maximizes overall performance and longevity in operation of the aiming eye. This is typically accomplished with an occluder on or in front of a shooter's shooting glasses. The occluder is usually hinged so that it can be positioned in front of the eye only when it's needed and otherwise rotated out of the field of vision when not in use. A field-expedient option that performs similarly is to place a small strip of opaque tape over the lens of the shooting glasses, limiting the visual information recognized by the non-aiming eye. If tape is not available, ChapStick or a light grease smeared on the lens of the non-aiming eye will perform the necessary action of allowing light to pass through but limiting the visual detail entering the eye.

An important fact to remember when diagnosing and troubleshooting vision issues pertaining to both the dominant eye and the non-dominant eye is that eye dominance is not consistent in all people. Although debated in some circles, there are some people who have eyes so closely matched that eye dominance changes with the introduction of stress, strain or fatigue. This phenomenon can be beneficial when it's appropriate for such a shooter to focus on the target in close and rapidly unfolding events, and it is easily controlled by limiting the amount of information entering the eye opposite of the hand controlling the trigger. All it takes is a squint or partial closure of the eye on the non-dominant side to shift eye dominance to the side controlling the gun.

LACK OF VISUAL CLARITY

Many shooters do not understand what they really need to see in order to achieve their desired results. The answer can vary with circumstance, target size, speed of shot delivery, distance to the target and a host of other variables.

When it comes to a handgun equipped with iron sights, a shooter needs to see contrast and reference in order to effectively engage a target. The contrast is so that a shooter can distinguish the difference between the rear sight, the front sight and the target. Even an aged-eye shooter who sees a hazy front and rear sight that are indistinguishable from one another (Figure 1) can resolve this by opening the rear-sight notch sufficiently to allow the aiming eye to differentiate and center the fuzzy front sight in the fuzzy rear-sight notch (Figure 2), providing a functional level of sight alignment. The eye will automatically center the front sight with unexpected precision as it is viewed through the

FIGURE 1

FIGURE 2

window of the rear-sight notch. The shooter only needs to recognize the target as a shape suitable for shooting. The eye will automatically find the center of the target, regardless of its shape, allowing the shooter to superimpose the fuzzy but aligned sights over the target's center. All that is left for the shooter to do is pull the trigger without affecting the sight-target relationship. Hits on target will be the result. Sometimes a shooter will use a field expedient, such as painting the sights different colors, to distinguish one from the other and both from the target to achieve a similar effect.

By understanding and utilizing the concept of contrast in seeing the difference between both sights and the target (in addition to using the center of the shape of the target rather than a specific spot on the target as a reference), a shooter complaining of the inability to see what he or she perceives as proper sight alignment, sight picture or both will find overall shooting performance renewed and improved. This method creates acceptable groups for most shooters — barring any other deficiencies that might affect their performance. By moving the sights to correspond with the desired point of impact on the target, the groups will move to the desired location.

MINI RED-DOT SIGHTS

With the advent of the mini red-dot sight (MRDS), a different set of parameters has arisen with its use, which has created more issues to diagnose and correct.

The MRDS is an alternative sighting system designed to benefit the shooter with a simplified and favorable visual input. In many cases, the MRDS user realizes there is a speed and accuracy advantage over the fa-

miliar conventional iron sights found on most handguns. In particular, someone with aged eyes or eye deficiencies affecting focal distances will generally benefit from using an MRDS to simplify the sight picture.

Consider that there is only one sight, the dot, to align with the target for an acceptable sight picture with an MRDS as opposed to the front and rear sights of a pistol with standard iron sights. Sight picture with an MRDS can be confusing when it comes to where a shooter's eyes should be focused to get the desired hit on the target.

There are two schools of thought as to where a shooter's eyes should be focused. Both have merit, and both are effective. The first focuses the aiming eye on the dot with the same intensity as a shooter would have on the front sight of an iron-sighted gun. In this case, the dominant eye is doing most of the work concentrating on the dot. The second provides a distinct advantage of the MRDS in that it allows the shooter to look at the target with both eyes as the dot is superimposed over the area of intended impact. Eye focus is the opposite from one to the other.

The best option is for a shooter to try both and favor the one that results in the best performance. However, a shooter should be familiar with both methods. From a tactical or hunting perspective, focusing on the desired point of impact while superimposing the red dot on that area as the shooter pulls trigger makes a lot of sense, all things considered.

As long as the shooter sees the dot on the target, whether focusing on the dot or the target, hits will occur. It is imperative that eye focus is hard on one or the other because when the eye focus wanders from its intended location, performance diminishes.

An additional diagnostic technique is to help the shooter find the dot from the holster on the way to the target.

Often, a first-time shooter using an MRDS will spend precious time locating the red dot on the screen and then getting it on target from the draw. More often than not, this makes the first-shot-on-target capability slower than the shooter can achieve with more-familiar iron sights. A big complaint about the MRDS is that the red dot is always on the top of the screen or even higher when a shooter draws to a target.

There are two simple ways to overcome this deficiency, which can be combined or used independently.

The first is primarily visual in nature. By using the backup iron sights initially as a reference in getting the muzzle on the target, the shooter will find that the co-witnessed red dot comes into view during the draw and presentation to the target. This makes it easier for the shooter to visually pick up the dot and get it on the target as he or she pulls the trigger. In short order, the shooter's primary focus will transition from the iron sights to the red dot, leaving the iron sights as a secondary point of reference in the visual field if needed.

The second method combines visual focus on the target with the physical movement of drawing from the holster to the target. The shooter accomplishes this by practicing the draw to the target slowly enough to get the "feel" (position) of the arms and hands in relation to the eyes necessary to get the dot on the target in the most direct manner. Doing this dry at first is beneficial because it isolates the action to only what is visually necessary to accomplish the task of effectively getting the dot on the target. Therefore, the shooter is conditioning the body to respond naturally and automatically to get the gun on target expediently and the dot where the eye is looking. Once the dry work is satisfactory in helping the shooter to get the dot on the target without having to search for it, live-fire can follow to validate the process. In many cases, this improves a shooter's skill level in speed and accuracy by fine-tuning both the draw and the presentation.

The perfect time for a shooter to optimize dot size and brightness for the intended application is while practicing drawing to the target. Many shooters will start with a small dot of 3 MOA or even less because that's what they have on their long guns. For a handgun, bigger is better because the apparent movement of the gun on the target is reduced with the bigger dot, which negates the hesitation to shoot because of the perceived movement. A shooter who is looking at the target can recognize the bigger dot much more easily and stabilize it more perceptually than a tiny pinpoint of light. Even a 6-, 8- or 10-MOA dot will yield surprising results. A larger dot is easier to find in varying light conditions as well. The brightness factor is often a battle between glaring and hard to find. Bigger and brighter are most useful when time is the major concern. For absolute precision, some prefer a smaller dot. As with where to focus the eyes, use the option that closest fits the need, but know and practice both applications.

Addressing these issues when a shooter is transitioning to an MRDS will save time in diagnosing and eliminating trouble spots in the beginning and maximizing performance immediately with the new equipment.

PHYSIOLOGICAL AND PSYCHOLOGICAL CONSIDERATIONS

Breathing is one of those things that all humans must do to stay alive. However, in shooting, there are many opinions as to when breathing should occur to optimize the delivery of the shot. There are as many variables as there are opinions on when and how to breathe.

Troubleshooting breathing concerns for a shooter practicing any discipline can be distilled down to stabilizing the muzzle on the target. It's a simple test that anyone can administer. The shooter should find a comfortable spot, remaining as still as possible for the few seconds it takes to fire a shot or string of shots. Odds are that when a shooter tries to eliminate as much motion from the body as possible — thereby maximizing the body's stability — he or she will find a comfort-

able spot in the breathing cycle to stop for the allotted time without giving it a thought. Breathing automatically resumes once the shooter no longer needs to be as motionless as possible. The thought of stabilizing the muzzle on the target as the shooter pulls the trigger until discharge takes place will take care of breathing in most every shooting application.

Sometimes competitive shooters will take partial breaths between shots to refresh their eyes and stay mentally focused when they are shooting prolonged strings of fire. Others might condition themselves to maintain their breathing to a specific time frame — sufficient to shooting their shots — before disturbing muzzle stability.

Either method is effective as long as breathing does not add motion to the muzzle when a shooter is firing.

Mental mistakes, by far, take precedence over biomechanical or visual errors in causing an individual's performance deficiencies in shooting. Loss of focus, emotional letdown or whatever an individual wants to name it comes from lack of planning and preparation as well as not having the discipline necessary to fully execute the skills currently in place. Negative thoughts, if allowed to permeate the mind, become self-fulfilling prophecies, degrading a shooter's performance.

Mental mistakes can be divided into the categories of the conscious and subconscious minds, although there is often some overlap between the two. Consciously ignoring logic and indisputable facts contributes to many of the mental lapses that a shooter encounters.

The objective of shooting is to hit the target. In order to hit the target, the shooter has to stabilize the muzzle on the target and pull the trigger without affecting the muzzle's stability to meet the objective. This is indisputable and must happen with every shot, no matter how quickly or slowly those shots are fired. It is that simple.

A major mental problem, especially for a new shooter, is fear of failure. Fear of failure is the lack of confidence in one's ability to perform to the perceived expectation that the individual or others have regarding his or her level of performance. Fear is an unnecessary emotion that is related to something that is perceived but rarely realized.

The mind tends to look for the worst possible outcome, which rarely ever occurs. Realistically and logically speaking, everyone has limitations. Keeping things in perspective, the body will not go where the mind has not been. Added to that perspective is that the body achieves what the mind believes. Keeping a positive, can-do outlook has brought success to more than one person in an undesirable situation.

"THE BODY ACHIEVES WHAT THE MIND BELIEVES."

When an individual exhibits a performance resulting in a personal best and yet falls short of personal expectations, is that a success or a failure? Sometimes weighing reality and objectivity in viewing one's performance diminishes the fear of failure since what a shooter sees is often better than expected.

A shooter can overcome a lack of confidence by assessing the challenge as it is presented and by simplifying the tasks to techniques previously learned. Confidence comes from knowing and being able to perform a task or tasks on demand, with minimal thought, and evolves to action without conscious thought, triggered through predetermined cues.

When improving a technique or action, a shooter may find it helpful to revisit the questions answered and actions performed when he or she originally learned it. The conscious mind must understand and accept the answers to the questions. What is the task? Why is this beneficial? How is this task done with the highest degree of efficiency and effectiveness? The shooter should then follow these questions with a review of previous performances in executing the task. Once this is mentally processed by the conscious mind and successfully performed visually and biomechanically, the shooter will establish confidence in the technique. Repetition, with attention to detail and efficiency in action, or eliminating errant movement, creates a subconscious action that responds to specific cues without conscious thought and increases speed of operation.

Simplicity in thought and action breeds success when challenges arise. Advanced shooting skills are nothing more than the basics performed in the most efficient and effective manner possible.

Converting conscious action to subconscious action is creating a habit that responds to a specific stimulus. Conscious repetition, exercised in the most precise and efficient manner possible, builds the habit and increases the speed of performance through economy of motion. Added to the action are the previously addressed answers of what, why and how, programming the subconscious brain to respond instantly when the appropriate stimulus occurs.

Controlling the emotional mind is one of the greatest challenges anyone will have to face in life. The emotional mind is associated with the subconscious mind in generating instant responses to stimuli that can sometimes be troublesome if not controlled or suppressed. The emotional disappointment of firing a bad shot will affect future shots until a shooter is able to get negative emotions under control sufficiently to continue without further effect. Negative emotions, such as hate, disappointment, intimidation, embarrassment and even fear, can gravely affect a shooter's performance. Even positive emotions such as elation, love and overconfidence can be detrimental to a shooter's performance. Any emotion that takes away from the focus and effort necessary to perform at the highest level is not in the best interest of the shooter striving for maximum performance.

A shooter can use the cognitive mind to control emotional interference through the use of logic, reason and the recognition of reality. Any factor beyond a shooter's control, such as the weather or an unanticipated distraction, often stimulates emotional activity even though the individual knows there is absolutely nothing he or she can do to change it. The more quickly the issue is recognized for what it is, the more quickly the shooter can return to the plan and routine with minimal lost effort. This is a product of the conscious mind taking control until any distractions pass.

If a shooter makes a mistake for which he or she is solely to blame, the conscious mind must quickly step in and analyze what went wrong and what is needed to return the shooter to the expected performance.

This can take place in a short segment of time, but it must take place prior to the individual firing the next shot or odds are that additional shots of an unsatisfactory nature will occur. This typically will compound the problem into a vicious cycle until the shooter can bring the situation under control. Self-forgiveness is an important trait to cultivate in overcoming the emotional aspect of firing a bad shot. Accept what can't be changed and go back to following a plan that works.

QUICK FIXES TO MENTAL FAILURES

An example of a mental failure is firing multiple shots in quick succession while failing to hit the target. The quick fix is for the shooter to slow down, engage the conscious mind to apply the basic fundamentals and shoot only as quickly as he or she can consistently hit the target. The shooter should be patient with the trigger, endeavoring to operate it smoothly, without moving the muzzle, and look for the smoke and flash at the muzzle each time the gun fires. Consciously thinking about smoothly operating the trigger while stabilizing the muzzle on the target, rather than trying to make the shots go somewhere they are not, will bring the gun back on target. A shooter might find that self-talk, such as "float the dot and shoot the shot" or "pull the front sight with the trigger," is beneficial in a quick recovery when shot delivery is not proceeding as expected.

Another failure is trying too hard to make something happen. The harder a shooter tries to hit a target, the less likely that will happen with any degree of consistency. Trying harder usually equates to using force to accomplish an end. Force causes muscle tension, hindering smooth movement and degrading stability of the muzzle in relation to the target. This detracts from consistent and accurate shooting.

When shooting is not going as smoothly as a shooter would prefer, the fix is to have a predetermined, proven plan that can be performed on demand. It can be something as simple as "A, B, C" or "1, 2, 3," with two to three steps to get the mind, body and eyes coordinated and reengaged. Executing the fundamentals of shot delivery and conscious thought through every step of the process will yield positive results. This coaching self-talk will help to eliminate distractions and keep the shooter's focus only on the immediate performance.

If time and circumstances permit, a shooter should strive to visualize the execution of the plan with enough detail so that the conscious mind is primed and comfortable in performing the preplanned event. It is helpful to simplify the plan to the minimum number of steps that are essential to delivering the desired shot (for instance, something as simple as putting the sights on the target and the finger on the trigger and pulling the front sight through the rear-sight window with the trigger movement until the smoke and flash can be seen at the muzzle).

The shooter can repeat as necessary. This occupies the shooter's brain, eyes and body simultaneously to help deliver the best performance possible, without distraction, under current conditions.

In the event of a distraction, internal or external, the shooter should have a reset point to which to return, which will allow him or her to follow the full mental plan to complete the shot.

In some disciplines of shooting, a shooter can minimize distractions by using double ear protection to cope with noise. A brimmed hat and blinders, occluders, side shields or other attachments to the shooting glasses will help to minimize visual distractions. Proper clothing to maximize comfort in the prevailing weather conditions will help to attenuate physical discomfort while shooting. Hydration and a snack are also important to sustain performance levels in comfort, which a shooter should not overlook. A shooter should address anything that can interfere with executing the best shots possible.

A shooter might find it advantageous to be a little hungry while shooting — but not to the point where the hunger is distracting or causes a feeling of weakness. On the other hand, overeating tends to dull the senses and often contributes to loss of focus both mentally and visually. When it comes to the intake of food and liquids, moderation is a good suggestion. Water is essential to a shooter staying visually and physically fresh for longer periods of time.

The recipe for good performance is coordinating the mind, body and eyes with everything else that is required to meet the objective without anything unnecessary that interferes with that objective.

Simple is good.

CHAPTER 12
DRILLS TO ATTAIN & RETAIN PROFICIENCY

The drills and exercises associated with shooting and shooting-related activities are endless. In most cases, every drill or exercise has some merit other than making noise and sending lead downrange. Analyzing each drill's characteristics will help a shooter choose what is best for the intended application.

The types of drills can be broken down into five categories, each of which is determined by its intended outcome.

Skill-development drills introduce new information and techniques to a shooter. In formal instruction, these drills are listed in the course description under what a student will be able to do at the completion of the class.

Skill-sustainment drills reinforce and aid, through repetition and experience, the shooter's retention and refinement of the material learned from the skill-development drills.

Proficiency-improvement drills are similar to skill-sustainment drills but usually have added value by exposing a shooter to alternate methods of achieving an objective. This provides options from which a shooter can choose to achieve the best results.

Skill-assessment drills are used to measure the progress of a shooter as well as to detect and correct any deficiencies in shooting performance.

Qualification drills are similar to skill-assessment drills, but a notable difference is that the former measures a student's performance on demand, to a standard, and under specific time frames and guidelines.

Each of these categories may feature dry-fire drills as well as live-fire drills.

Dry-fire exercises replicate the mechanics of firing live ammunition — visually, physically and mentally — without the distraction of noise, recoil or other factors that may interfere with a shooter's plan of shot delivery.

Dry-fire drills are particularly effective in initializing and ingraining hard mechanical skills essential to marksmanship, gun-handling and self-diagnosing deficiencies in a shooter's delivery system. They also offer an aid to instructors and coaches in detecting and correcting imperfections in their shooters' shooting skill sets. Dry-fire drills should be a regular part of a shooter's regimen in maintaining and improving previously learned skills. In fact, it is not uncommon for an advanced-level precision shooter to dry-fire upwards of 50 dry pulls of the trigger for each one of the live-fire shots.

Live-fire drills are where a shooter puts previously acquired knowledge and skill into practical application with a gun and ammunition.

Every drill a shooter adopts should coincide with a particular goal. If it does not add value to the shooter's overall plan, the exercise is little more than a waste of time and ammunition. It can even cause bad habits along

1 SKILL-DEVELOPMENT
INTRODUCES NEW INFORMATION AND TECHNIQUES TO A SHOOTER

2 SKILL-SUSTAINMENT
REINFORCES AND AIDS IN THE RETENTION AND REFINEMENT OF SKILLS

3 PROFICIENCY-IMPROVEMENT
EXPOSES A SHOOTER TO ALTERNATE METHODS OF ACHIEVING AN OBJECTIVE

4 SKILL-ASSESSMENT
MEASURES THE PROGRESS OF A SHOOTER AND DETECTS AND CORRECTS ANY DEFICIENCIES

5 QUALIFICATION
MEASURES A STUDENT'S PERFORMANCE, INCORPORATING SPECIFIC TIME FRAMES OR OTHER FACTORS

the way. By starting with a specific objective, a shooter can create a clear pathway to success. Methods can change so long as the original objective is met. If, however, the objective changes, it may take the shooter several tries to nail down what must be accomplished to meet that objective. Either way, flexibility is important in ensuring a shooter ends up with the best results.

Unless unlimited time, money and ammunition change the equation, it is prudent for a shooter to be selective in what activities are most beneficial to pursue. Starting with simple objectives and reasonable expectations is the best way to get the most reward with the least amount of effort.

Initially, building a good foundation of safety, gun nomenclature, gun-handling and basic marksmanship will provide a launching point for more specific endeavors, such as personal defense, competitive shooting, hunting and any other undertaking involving a firearm.

Perhaps the most important question a shooter should ask when selecting a drill is why the drill is the most beneficial for achieving a particular goal. If more than one answer presents itself, there is nothing wrong with trying several drills. It will become evident which drill best meets the shooter's objective.

The primary objective of shooting, regardless of discipline, is to hit the target. A shooter must start by learning to stabilize the muzzle of the gun on the target using previously learned attributes such as body position, grip and minimal tension in the body. Then a shooter can move on to pulling the trigger to fire the shot in a manner that has no effect on the muzzle's stability relative to the target. It is easier said than done. But these are the two essentials for each and every shot to be successful in hitting the target.

Above all else, stabilizing the muzzle on the target and operating the trigger to fire the gun without affecting that stability are the foundations on which every shooter, no matter the discipline, should build to achieve success.

WALL DRILL

The "Wall Drill," mentioned throughout this book, is the foundational drill to condition the eyes, hands and brain to coordinate in maximizing an individual's shooting performance with the least amount of effort.

The drill not only propagates good follow-through habits but also reveals deficiencies in grip and trigger manipulation. Along with improving visual and biomechanical factors, the drill conditions the shooter's brain to signal the trigger finger to pull the trigger without conscious thought when the eye views the desired sight picture. This condition formulates the purest form of shot release — with the eyes, hands and brain working together on a subconscious plane (better known as being "in the zone").

A major benefit of the "Wall Drill" is that it eliminates unnecessary distractions. It conditions a shooter to concentrate only on the necessities required to fire an acceptable shot, which minimizes the steps needed for the best performance.

A shooter can practice the "Wall Drill" with any firearm that is equipped with sights designed for precision shot placement on a target. This includes using a rifle, shotgun, pistol or revolver from any position that provides a stable platform.

It is unique in that it features everything a shooter needs to shoot accurately and removes anything that is not absolutely necessary.

Movement of the front sight or gun when the shooter pulls the trigger signifies that there are deficiencies in the shot-delivery system that need to be corrected. Any time there is movement, there is movement of the muzzle's position on the target. Misaligning the sights or mismanipulating the trigger prior to the bullet's exit from the muzzle usually yields undesirable results.

A good course of action to follow when practicing the "Wall Drill" is to fire five practice shots, taking notice of any deficiencies during the cycle. If any deficiency is apparent, a shooter should correct it by making a change to what caused the deficiency. The change can be validated by repeating the drill.

Once the "Wall Drill" can be performed satisfactorily and consistently, the shooter will be able to perform live-fire exercises with success.

The "Wall Drill" is the foundation of accurate shooting. It can be used to diagnose and improve deficiencies in a shooter's performance. All shooters should practice it regularly to maintain an edge in their chosen shooting disciplines. The "Wall Drill" is the pathway to maintaining sharp focus on the sights and a high level of coordination between the eyes, hands and brain.

BULLET HOLE DRILL

There are several variants of the "Bullet Hole Drill," all of which essentially validate the "Wall Drill" with live-fire.

Typically, the "Bullet Hole Drill" uses a blank target at 3 yards. A shooter can use any serviceable gun and ammunition to fire the drill. For best results, the shooter should fire a minimum of five shots while performing this drill. (The shooter can fire more shots, but keeping the round count low makes shot-performance analysis more accurate.) The "Bullet Hole Drill" is most often performed standing and with both hands. Any drill practiced with the "Wall Drill" can be completed with the "Bullet Hole Drill" as well.

The shooter's first shot through the target becomes the point of reference for the rest of the shot string. Ideally, subsequent shots will pass through the same hole, indicating that the shooter's eyes, hands and brain are working together as they should.

The shot impact can depend on the ammunition and how the sights on the gun are zeroed. It is not uncommon for a shooter's subsequent shots, after that first reference shot, to impact in a slightly different location on the target. Even if they do impact in a different location, the subsequent shots should be tightly clustered or touch in one hole to provide the desired outcome.

An alternate way to fire the "Bullet Hole Drill" is to use a sheet of printer paper or a small paper plate as the target. Putting the aligned sights on the perceived center of the target, the shooter should execute the smoothest trigger pull possible to break the shot and then shoot four more shots using the same target hold and technique. All shots should be touching, if not in the same hole.

This method of firing the "Bullet Hole Drill" exemplifies the ability of the eye to precisely find the center of an object consistently. Additional value in using this method is that it promotes hard focus on the sights instead of a specific spot on the target. If there were a specific spot on the target on which to hold, it could distract and cause the shooter to glance at the target while pulling the trigger, which would negatively affect the desired result. The eye does all the work by keeping the sights centered on the target and the hits in a tight group.

A spin-off of holding the aligned sights on the center of a paper plate or piece of printer paper is shooting a target that has an irregular shape and no specific aiming point. By seeing the aligned sights on the center of the shape of the object and smoothly operating the trigger, a shooter virtually guarantees a hit.

SHOOT THE SHAPE DRILL

The "Shoot the Shape Drill," described in Chapter 11, is particularly applicable in personal-defense situations, hunting or competition, where only partial or irregular targets are available to a shooter and there is no "X" to mark the spot of impact.

The drill benefits a shooter when target distance increases or the appearance of the target size decreases. This is because there is less obvious movement of the sights on the target as opposed to trying to hold on a specific spot, which often induces the shooter to peek at the target to verify the hold on the target. Any time the eye focus leaves the front sight prior to the bullet exiting the muzzle, a miss is likely to occur. The "Shoot the Shape Drill" simplifies shooting accurately and consistently by allowing the shooter to concentrate on the fundamentals without having to cope with any distractions.

WALK BACK DRILL

A follow-on drill to the "Bullet Hole Drill" and the "Shoot the Shape Drill" is the "Walk Back Drill." The "Walk Back Drill" can start as the "Bullet Hole Drill" at 3 yards with an initial five-shot group. A shooter will fire the next five-shot group after increasing distance from the

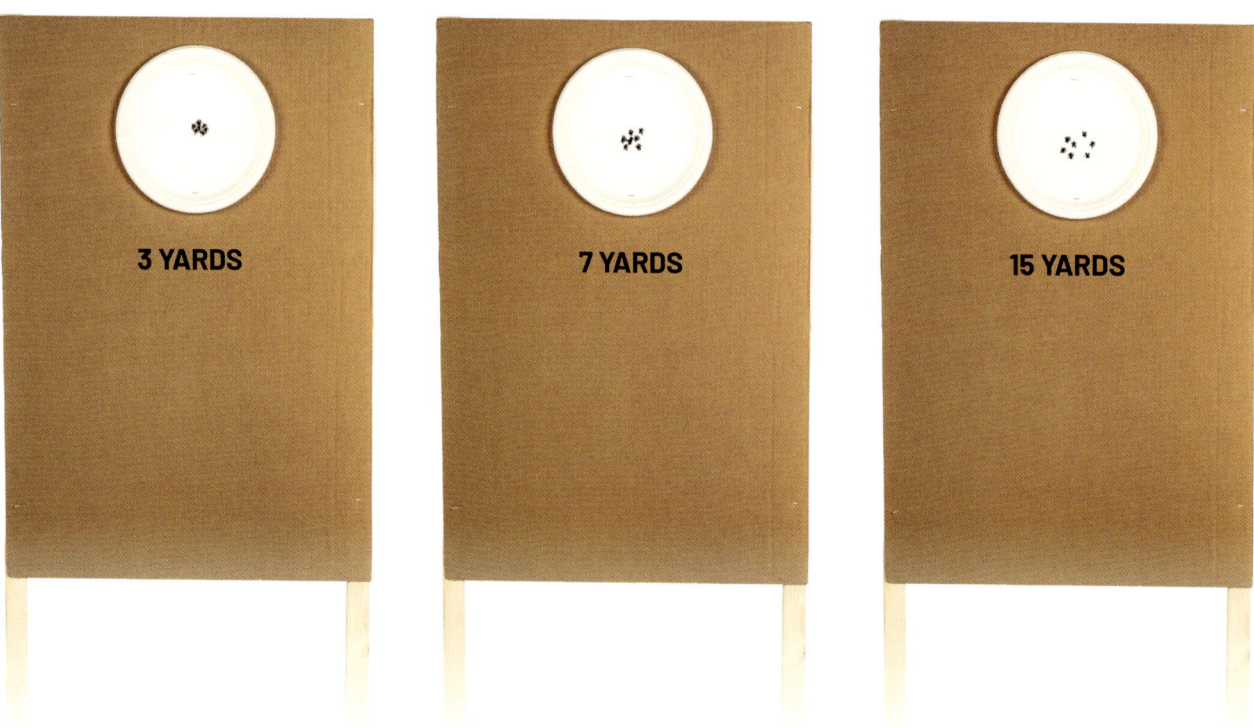

target an additional 3 yards. The shooter will fire each subsequent five-shot group after increasing the target distance another 3 yards. A box of 50 rounds of ammunition will allow the shooter to fire, in 3-yard increments, back to 30 yards. While 30 yards may be a goal to work toward, it is not unreasonable to move back to 50 or even 100 yards or further to test and validate a shooter's marksmanship skills.

The goal is for the shooter to keep all shots in an 8-inch circle from start to finish. The 8-inch circle is relevant in that it's similar to the center zone of targets used in competitive shooting, the heart or lung area of a medium-to-large game animal, and the upper-center mass of the chest area of a human adversary in a lethal-force confrontation.

The "Walk Back Drill" helps to build marksmanship skills and diagnose deficiencies in shooter performance — particularly when distance is added to the equation.

It is an excellent drill to detect a shooter's eye focus drifting toward the target as the distance increases. Usually after the 9- to 12-yard marks, shots start to drift below the 8-inch target and get lower as the distance increases. This is because the shooter is looking over the sights at the target to see where and if shots are impacting. The muzzle then points lower, causing the impacts to hit lower.

An easy way to remedy shooting lower on the target as the distance increases is to employ the sight-picture method used in the "Shoot the Shape Drill." Have the shooter align the sights, with hard eye focus on the front sight, on the center of the entire target and pull the trigger. Be sure the shooter is observing the smoke and flash at the muzzle to verify eye focus is where it should be for each of the five shots. It is important that the shooter have the discipline to wait until all shots have been fired and only then observe the target. The group will be in the middle with the rest of the shots, where it should be.

The "Walk Back Drill" can be used at any realistic distance, depending on the gun and ammunition the shooter is using. Distance can be gauged by the maximum distance of the intended application and the capability of the equipment used.

RESET DRILL

When a shooter is firing multiple shots in rapid succession, the "Reset Drill" can help lay the groundwork for shooting those shots in the most efficient manner possible.

It is best for a shooter to initially practice the "Reset Drill" in steps. This allows the shooter to experience the feel of the recoil as the muzzle rises off the target, the movement of the trigger — both forward and rearward — and the recovery to the target coordinated into a smooth flow of shots without unnecessary motion during the firing sequence.

The "Reset Drill" starts with a shooter aiming and firing one shot at a target. As the bullet exits the muzzle, the gun lifts off the target in recoil. At or before the peak of the recoil arc, the shooter releases the trigger forward to the point of reset. As the gun settles back to its original position, the shooter applies pressure to the trigger, coordinating to release the next shot at the instant the muzzle is back on the target. The shooter can repeat this sequence as necessary until he or she fires the desired number of shots or depletes the ammunition supply.

It is important that the shooter follow these steps without using unnecessary force on the gun in recovery to the target or elsewhere since it is detrimental to the timing and flow of the shot delivery. Smooth operation of the trigger in each direction is critical to the successful implementation of the "Reset Drill." Once the shooter's trigger finger coordinates with the rise and fall of the muzzle, the individual can fire accurate shots as quickly as the eye can recognize the sight picture necessary to hit the next target.

Trigger control is the key to all shooting disciplines — especially when it comes to precision marksmanship. Very often, time may be a factor in delivering an accurate shot. This leads to a shooter operating the trigger as quickly as possible while having minimal-to-no impact on the gun's stability on the target.

NOW DRILL

The "Now Drill," sometimes referred to as a "command detonation exercise," is a training method of conditioning the trigger finger to move the trigger on demand, independent of the rest of the body. It is often described as a shooter "being patient with the trigger in a hurry."

The signal to fire can be audible, visual or both during this drill. The shooter should begin the drill expecting a signal to fire and knowing the proper response to the signal. This helps to prevent an erratic

response to the fire command, which often moves the gun along with the trigger.

In the beginning, practicing the "Now Drill" dry in concert with the "Wall Drill" minimizes the stimuli for a shooter to comprehend and manage. Once the shooter can consistently pull the trigger on demand without adding motion to the gun, the transition to live-fire comes next.

Live-fire for the "Now Drill" does not have to be complicated. All that is required is a gun, ammunition and a target with a suitable backstop. An electronic timer is helpful to give the signal to fire and to measure the speed with which the shooter can fire the shot. (While helpful, it is not essential, as time is only a portion of measuring success.)

A good starting point for a shooter new to the concept is to place an 8-inch paper plate in the middle of a cardboard backer at 3 yards. When ready, the shooter can load the gun and assume a comfortable shooting position — finger on the trigger — aiming at the plate and waiting for the signal to fire. When the signal to fire occurs, the shooter's initial goal is to hit the plate in one second or less with one shot. As a shooter's proficiency and skill improve, times should be shortened (or distances can be increased) to further the challenge of shooting an accurate shot on demand in a minimum amount of time.

Another component beneficial to the shooter when practicing the "Now Drill" is varying the signal to fire from audible to visual, such as a target that appears and disappears in a narrow time frame or a flash of light, perhaps with colors that signify some type of action. Varying the stimuli will condition the shooter to maintain full attention on the exercise, which is essential for maximum performance.

PRECISION TO POINT TRANSITION DRILL

The "Precision to Point Transition Drill" is a valuable drill in guiding a shooter to fire with the accuracy necessary in the least amount of time possible. It incorporates the shooter's natural eye-hand coordination with the input of variable sight pictures as the shooter smoothly operates the trigger to put accurate shots on target.

The basic guideline comes from the target as it appears in relation to the outline of the gun aimed at the target.

If the outline of the gun is encompassed by the outline of the target, the eye will center the gun on the target, allowing for hits near the middle — provided the shooter operates the trigger without creating excess motion to the muzzle. This mitigates a shooter needing to find and align the sights on the target before pulling the trigger and, therefore, saves time. If a shooter can see the outline of the slide or cylinder within the outline of the target, he or she should be able to place shots in the middle of the target using the eye's natural ability to center objects.

If the outline of the gun appears larger than the outline of the target, that indicates the shooter should incorporate the sights for the best results in accurate shooting.

These general guidelines may vary from shooter to shooter.

The drill is simple to set up and employ. As an example, a full-sized qualification or competition target can be used effectively. The drill is best performed dry initially to maximize the visual recognition of the gun in relation to the target at the various distances.

The shooter should begin at 3 yards and observe the appearance of the gun falling within the outline of the target while aiming for center. The shooter can continue with the "Walk Back Drill," noticing at each distance how the outline of the gun relates to the outline of the target. A shooter might find that the outline of the gun and the outline of the target are similar in the 10- to 12-yard range. As distance increases, the outline of the gun will appear to be larger than the outline of the target. Once the gun's outline obscures the target, that is the visual signal that a more precise sight picture is required, and the shooter will need to employ the sights with a more conventional sight picture.

A shooter should practice the drill live-fire at specific known distances at first to reinforce the visual input of when to transition from precision shooting to point shooting and back again. Validation is measured by the resulting hits on target.

Once a shooter builds confidence with this technique, it becomes apparent that the size of the target or the distance from the target — or both — will provide the visual input to dictate whether the individual can just point the gun at the target and pull the trigger to make the necessary hits or if the shooter must take time to acquire a conventional sight picture to deliver the hits required.

With practice, the shooter will be able to determine the level of speed and accuracy necessary to engage a target by visual input.

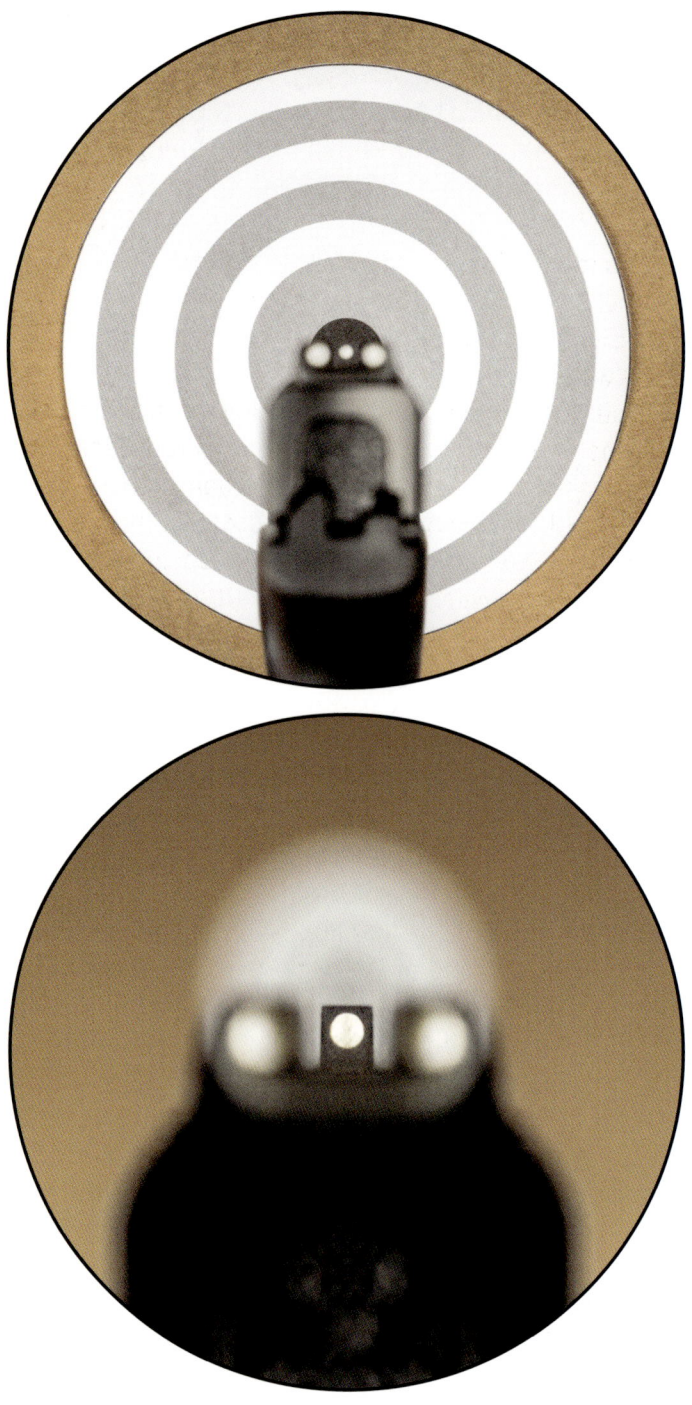

ONE-HANDED SHOOTING DRILLS

One-handed shooting drills are often overlooked because they are more difficult to perform successfully than with two hands working in unison.

Though a lot of shooters may think of shooting with one hand as a nice skill to attain, many deem the skill unnecessary to accomplish their goals. They may think that since they have two hands, why not use them?

A competitive shooter, depending on the particular discipline, may find it necessary to either shoot with one hand to compete within the rules of the game or to engage targets with the strong or support hand only due to the conditions and requirements of the competition.

Someone who carries for personal defense has a greater investment in learning and becoming proficient in one-handed skills than the casual or competitive shooter. This is because there are no hard and fast rules that come into play during a justified gunfight. There is a general consensus of thought in some circles that an individual who ends up in a dynamic personal-defense confrontation will more likely than not have to engage an assailant with only one hand.

Being able to shoot with one hand is especially beneficial if an individual is injured or has only hand available due to the immediate circumstance. But perhaps one of the greatest benefits is helping the shooter to refine his or her overall skill set to an even higher level of achievement.

From a physical perspective, practicing dry and shooting with one hand strengthens muscles needed to shoot successfully when there is no longer support from the opposite hand. Equally as important is isolating finger pressure on the gun so that the gripping fingers and the trigger finger operate independently and consistently.

Placement of the thumb on the grip will likely change from what was used with two hands in order to provide support to the area left vacant by the missing hand. A shooter might find it beneficial to contact the gripping fingers with the thumb (if hand size permits). This will provide a full encirclement of the grip in order for the shooter to better control the recoil of the gun during firing. Even with this method of gripping the pistol, the angle and distance the gun rises and settles on the target is likely to be different from when a shooter uses two hands.

When shooting one-handed, a shooter must acclimate to visually tracking the gun through recoil and recovery to the target, which will require some effort. Depending on a shooter's eye dominance, the relationship between how the shooter holds the gun and how it is seen by the eye for the desired sight picture — translated into the head's position in relation to the gun — will likely have to change in order for the shooter to achieve optimal performance.

The psychological factor of shooting one-handed is significant in that logic dictates that two is always better than one. This thought process tends to sharpen both focus and attention to detail in shot delivery when a shooter is using one hand in order to obtain the best results with the available assets. Once this mental habit is in place, a shooter can apply it while shooting with both hands as well.

Every drill a shooter practices with two hands can and should be repeated with one hand.

SUPPORT-HAND-ONLY DRILLS

Once a shooter establishes proficiency with the dominant hand only, further development in marksmanship ability can be brought forth by employing the non-dominant or support hand.

Support-hand-only drills require focus and attention to detail in order for a shooter to handle and manipulate a gun. This can feel like uncharted territory — and even like learning how to shoot all over again.

Even though a shooter knows how to execute a task from the other side of the body, it still requires conscious thought during physical performance because it is new information that must be downloaded into the subcon-

scious mind. This conscious thought provides an overall review and validation of what information the shooter previously learned, including how it was applied on the dominant side. The learning process in shooting from the support side always enhances the mental performance, which carries over to the strong side, where a shooter is more proficient and comfortable. The confidence generated by being able to perform at an acceptable level with either hand is immeasurable.

When learning to operate a handgun with one hand only, a shooter must revisit the size of the gun compared to the size of the hand. Deficiencies masked by the use of two hands in shooting become apparent when only one hand is available to operate the gun. Recoil alone may be a serious factor when multiple shots are required. This in itself may cause a shooter to reevaluate the caliber and power level of the gun carried for personal defense. The shooter should be able to control the gun and be able to put multiple hits on target with either hand on demand.

Grip circumference and trigger reach are primary considerations, although a shooter cannot ignore the operation of other control features of a gun. This applies to both hands since there are no guarantees that one or the other will be available at any given time. Be aware that dexterity, strength, range of motion and even size may be different from one hand to the other. There may have to be compromises to find the best option. Trigger manipulation trumps everything else because the muzzle must stay on the target until the bullet exits the muzzle in order to achieve a hit. When the act of pulling the trigger causes the muzzle to deviate from the point of aim, success will not be realized. Practicing the "Wall Drill" with either hand alone will validate a shooter's proper trigger control or the need for improvement.

Ideally, the gun should function as an extension of the shooter's hand, including the ability to operate all of the controls with either hand without a shift of the grip.

One-hand-only shooting drills not only are practical and necessary but also reinforce — visually, mentally and physically — every fundamental required to shoot accurately and successfully.

TWO PRIMARY TENETS

The preceding drills are provided as guidelines to improve a shooter's marksmanship skills, regardless of his or her reason for shooting. These drills incorporate the three attributes that a shooter must possess and put into application in order to consistently shoot acceptable shots.

The blend of visual input and biomechanical action, coordinated by the brain, cogitatively or subconsciously, are the essentials needed for successful and enjoyable shooting. A shooter can refine and reinforce marksmanship skills by practicing these exercises, both in dry- and live-fire, on a regular and continuous basis. Once the shooter is familiar with the physical aspects of a drill, his or her mental imagery will aid in the progression for improvement.

Ultimately, every drill listed in this chapter, and any other drills that a shooter might encounter pertaining to marksmanship, can be distilled down to two components that must be employed by the shooter to maximize the potential for success: muzzle management and trigger-finger discipline.

A shooter who practices these will achieve the two primary tenets of shooting, which are safety and success.

CHAPTER 13

PATHS TO IMPROVEMENT

Marksmanship is a lifelong and often life-changing endeavor that can be both challenging and rewarding. The reasons an individual shoots and the various approaches to shooting are nearly infinite.

No matter a shooter's progression over time or through multiple approaches, the foundational tenets of safety and success remain the same. It is both undeniable and indisputable that muzzle management and trigger-finger discipline provide safety and success.

The basis of all shooting, including marksmanship, starts with a safety and success mindset, closely followed by where to point the muzzle of the gun and how to address the trigger to consistently achieve both together.

A critical area that is often overlooked in the beginner's path to success is how to eliminate the fear of the noise and movement of the gun. The inoculation drills provide a simple means of overcoming this fear, which, if a shooter does not address, induces undesirable movement of the gun during firing. Overcoming this natural response to the sound and movement of the gun is imperative in relieving unnecessary distractions when a shooter is learning foundational shooting skills.

TRAINING APPROACH

One of the most effective means of streamlining a shooter's progress is through how information is communicated. Whether an instructor's lesson is academic or practical, simplicity in concept and action enhances a student's understanding and ability to reproduce it.

It is important to keep in mind throughout the training process that advanced techniques are little more than the basic techniques performed in the most efficient and effective manner. This emphasizes the importance of a strong foundation on which a shooter can build for future development.

A shooter learns better by following an objective-based training approach rather than a hard-and-fast guideline. This allows for individual progression as opposed to a one-size-fits-all concept. When a shooter realizes that there is usually more than one way to achieve a desired outcome, it opens the door for performance levels beyond his or her expectations.

Understanding and studying the three areas necessary to deliver the best shooting performance and how they interface with one another to provide the expected results is paramount to a shooter's progression, regardless of depth or discipline.

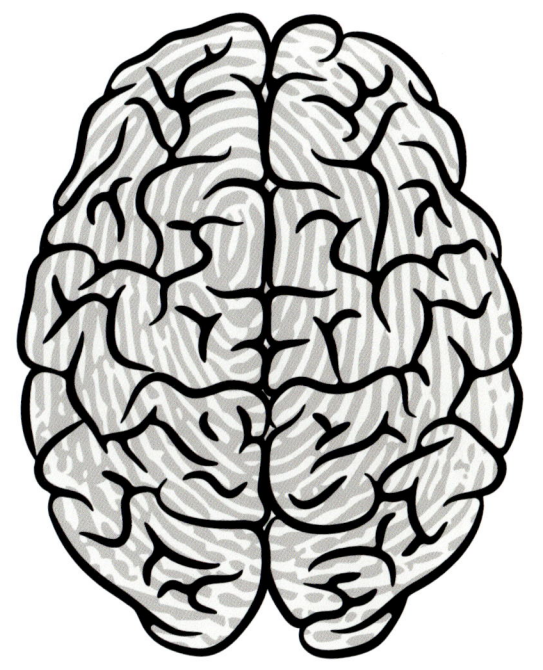

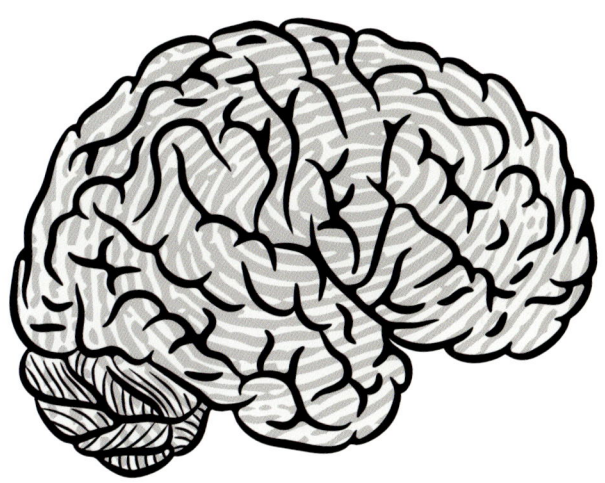

BRAIN, VISION AND BODY

Both the conscious and subconscious portions of the human brain are important contributors included in the triad of brain, vision and body. However, in many cases, the mental side of shooting is the least studied and understood. A shooter's progression begins at the cognitive (conscious) level of brain function. A thorough understanding of what the concept entails, why it is beneficial to the shooter, and how it is performed (with accuracy and through repetition) using the best methods programs the brain with desired information. Conscious repetition transitions what was once a diligent thought process that led to action to a subconscious, automatic response of accuracy and speed with a low probability of error.

Aside from an understanding of the brain and how it affects shooting performance, the eyes and how they function are at the next level of progression. Understanding human vision enhances a shooter's performance.

Learning and understanding how the eyes function to provide information to the brain will greatly improve a shooter's skills and execution. The concept of natural centering is a feature of human vision that, once realized, will greatly accelerate an individual's shooting performance. Eye dominance is variable and stronger in some shooters than others. Variable-focus shooting is another technique of combining central-vision input with peripheral-vision input to maximize hit probability when conditions are rapidly changing. The eyes take in much more information than the shooter consciously processes. Striving to cultivate a higher rate of selectivity from the visual stream will advance a shooter's ability to perform in significant leaps. There is no such thing as too much visual information — so long as it is classified correctly as it pertains to the immediate condition and does not create a distraction. Continual practice in maximizing the usefulness of visual input and identifying its value is essential to a shooter's progress.

Understanding the physical aspects of shooting at a foundational level is essential for the shooter to formulate a biomechanical baseline from which to build. One of the two things that a shooter must never forget concerning biomechanics is that not everybody is physically the same or has the same ability. Shooters have different ranges of motion, flexibility, strength, size and speed of movement, among other variables.

In developing grip, trigger manipulation, stance, natural point of aim, muzzle stability in different shooting positions, firing while moving and other biomechanical-related faculties, a shooter must focus on natural attributes and the economy of motion in optimizing performance as his or her ability evolves.

By revisiting the three components of shot delivery — mental, visual and physical — regularly, as well as studying how they interface with each other, a shooter can better understand what is essential for success. It will also help the shooter discern what may be nice to have as an option but isn't essential for overall performance.

DIVERSIFICATION

It is important for a shooter to diversify the interests that initially brought him or her to a particular shooting discipline. This diversification will reinvigorate the shooter by broadening the scope of developmental activities and providing a different perspective to help enhance any current skill sets.

Each discipline has its own set of rules and parameters that will add to a shooter's base knowledge, evolving from the concept of safety and success with the goal of consistently hitting the target. Even though a shooter can take many paths, the sequence of events will often be similar to the following guidelines.

Engaging in casual shooting is a fun way to start but has little relevance to improving a shooter's skills.

Taking a few entry-level classes from reputable trainers will help the novice shooter to determine the focus of future efforts. Diversifying the current skill set with classes that challenge a more advanced shooter with new disciplines will result in improvements to that shooter's overall ability.

Precision marksmanship is the epitome of the shooting disciplines in that it incorporates all of the fundamentals necessary to successfully hit a target. A shooter must understand that the speed with which he or she delivers shots will vary with the precision required. Here, a shooter learns that economy of motion will result in speed with accuracy. One of the primary takeaways when practicing speed and accuracy together is for the individual to shoot only as fast as he or she can make hits on the target.

Defensive shooting for personal protection builds on shooting for speed and accuracy in that different clothing and equipment are factored into the equation. In addition to the shooting skills already in place, tactical skills of improvised positions, movement, cover and concealment, irregular target engagement, and working in reduced light conditions — among many other variables — expand the shooter's progression toward a lifetime of learning opportunities.

Competitive shooting provides an excellent opportunity to practice and improve previously learned skills from both a marksmanship and tactical perspective. Learning to control the stress of competition helps a shooter to build confidence through achieving success

under pressure and enhances that shooter's ability to succeed in a combat encounter. It is important when progressing as a competitive shooter to differentiate between competition and combat shooting. The rules of engagement may be different even though the skills of engagement are very similar.

Although a relatively small number of shooters in the handgun fraternity consider hunting with a handgun, the few who do find that the skills necessary to be successful culminate from multiple disciplines. The skill to place a precision shot — in a fleeting moment under tremendous pressure and from an undesirable position or unfavorable environment — draws from every aspect of a shooter's training and ability to perform on demand. Notwithstanding, the tactical skills necessary to deliver an ethical shot with the equipment in hand further tests the skills acquired by the hunter.

The diversification of a shooter may ebb and flow as time and resources permit. However, it is important for the shooter to remain engaged with multiple disciplines in order for progression to continue meeting the challenges of skill improvement. Not doing so tends to cause stagnation, which stops progress in its tracks.

DETECTING DEFICIENCIES

The importance of having the best tools for the job at hand cannot be overstated. A shooter who engages and progresses in multiple shooting endeavors will quickly realize that one piece of equipment will not fit all applications. Even though guns, accessories and ammunition may be used for a variety of purposes, it comes down to the degree and depth in which a shooter wants to indulge in a particular discipline. Having the best equipment available or that's affordable will help a shooter achieve the highest level of results and will eliminate one variable of an excuse for an undesirable shot. Validation of the capabilities of a shooter's equipment helps to build confidence in that shooter. It forces the shooter to focus on his or her own performance instead of being distracted by mechanical variables that may or may not exist.

Having learned the foundational skills of marksmanship — what they entail, how and why they benefit the shooter, the methods of how and why they are performed and practiced, and why they are important for the shooter to know and be able to put into application — a shooter then has the preliminary skills to self-diagnose and troubleshoot any deficiencies.

Further study and practical experience lead to the ability to differentiate vision deficiencies from biomechanical failures or mental mistakes, allowing the shooter to address and find a solution to most any shooting problem.

At this juncture, a shooter possesses and understands the information necessary for creating and executing accurate shots on a target and also understands what may be the root cause of an issue, perhaps even recognizing a method for remedying the condition. A shooter who can self-diagnose and correct individual problems can also validate the condition and capability of firearms and ammunition as they pertain to a certain discipline.

This step of self-diagnosis is a major milestone in a shooter's progression and opens the door for the next steps on the journey to becoming an expert marksman.

PAY IT FORWARD

A major step in a shooter's progression is when the shooter is able to share knowledge and can demonstrate a technique to another shooter at a lower skill level. Being able to distill the subject matter down to the granular level so that it makes sense, is believable and is easy to reproduce makes transferring and retaining information easier. Remember: The simpler, the better.

This is a major component of what it takes to be a successful educator and trainer in almost any aspect of life — but especially with firearms.

Practice is always part of the progression of shooting because it is a perishable skill. It is beneficial for a shooter (as well as any observers) if a skill is demonstrated and performed correctly. Practicing a skill or series of skills to improve performance involves breaking down each movement and each visual input as they are being coordinated by the brain to ensure the efficiency and effectiveness of the action. If speed is a concern, it will come as a result of eliminating anything that is visually, physically or mentally unnecessary in achieving the desired result. Trying to force speed is futile since it almost always causes unnecessary tension in the body, resulting in the shooter exceeding his or her ability to hit the target with any degree of consistency.

When detecting and correcting identified flaws in a technique being practiced, a shooter should self-coach with the same analysis and advice that he or she would give to another shooter when assisting that shooter in addressing a similar problem.

Practicing what you preach not only reinforces personal performance in a positive manner but also sets the example for others to emulate.

There comes a time when a shooter has satisfied a good number of goals or objectives and is close to satisfaction with his or her level of skill and knowledge of the subjects. That does not mean that the individual automatically stops learning or revisiting material. And it certainly does not mean that the shooter has closed the door on self-improvement. It means that the shooter has met the original goals and can now gradually refocus both time and energy into mentoring others by sharing knowledge while still striving for personal excellence.

What comes next for a shooter is to perpetuate the shooting disciplines by inviting others to join in and enabling them to have a positive experience — especially in the initial stages of their newfound avocation.

"Pay it forward" is a phrase often used to describe a means of continuing a personal interest in a particular subject as new people are introduced into a fresh and different branch of knowledge.

One of the best ways to accomplish this is for a shooter to go back to the beginning of his or her journey and consider what elements furnished the greatest benefit and what elements were of little value. Typically, these can be divided into what makes sense and is easily reproduced. Information or techniques that were difficult to understand or not immediately applicable should be saved for further study. All information is of value when it's categorized properly. Some information applies to the job at hand, and some does not. The main thing is to stick with what is relevant and not become distracted with things that do not contribute to the current goal.

Sometimes this concept of sharing and helping others improve can become a passion to pursue and can mature further into instructing.

A shooter can enhance this endeavor (and learn to communicate more effectively) by enrolling in courses for instructors and shooting coaches. The individual can then follow this up by actually interacting with students in need of the newfound knowledge.

Many educators find that their best learning experiences come from when they are teaching others.

An objective-based approach simplifies the message and allows students to use their own natural attributes and thought processes to achieve success. And familiar analogies can help those individuals firmly lock learned information in place.

Along the road to self-improvement, a shooter may find that the memory and utilization of holistic techniques that combine biomechanical actions with visual input — merged and controlled by the brain — will help consistently generate a maximized level of performance.

Marksmanship and the many disciplines that encompass the safe and successful use of firearms provide a camaraderie of advocates, mentors, competitors and friendly rivals whose philosophies may be different but who all have a common thread in their support and exercising of the Second Amendment.

As representatives of the shooting sports and stalwart supporters of the legal use of firearms, we have a collective responsibility to perpetuate the skills and knowledge we have acquired — as well as the freedoms we enjoy — for generations to come.

NOTES